KANAZAWA

Recollections of a Living Karate Legend

The Early Years (1931-1964)

OTHER BOOKS BY CLIVE LAYTON

Conversations with Karate Masters
Unmasking the Martial Artist
Mysteries of the Martial Arts
Mind Training for the Martial Arts
Training with Funakoshi
Karate Master: The Life & Times of Mitsusuke Harada
Shotokan Dawn: Vol. I (in press)
Shotokan Dawn: Vol. II (in press)
A Shotokan Karate Book of Facts: Vol. I
A Shotokan Karate Book of Facts: Vol. II
A Shotokan Karate Book of Facts: Vol. III
The Kanazawa Years
Reminiscences by Master Mitsusuke Harada
A Shotokan Karate Book of Dates
The Shotokan Karate Book of Quotes
Funakoshi on Okinawa (in press)

KANAZAWA, 10th DAN

Recollections of a Living Karate Legend
The Early Years (1931-1964)

BY

DR. CLIVE LAYTON

SHOTO PUBLISHING

26 POYNTER ROAD, ENFIELD, MIDDLESEX, EN1 1DL, ENGLAND

First Published in 2001
by **Shoto Publishing**, 26 Poynter Road, Enfield,
Middlesex, EN1 1DL, ENGLAND
Tel: 020-8366-2282
www.shoto.org

Copyright © 2001 Clive Layton

All rights reserved. No part of this publication may be reproduced or transmitted in any form or by any means, electronic or mechanical, including photocopying, recording, or by any information storage and retrieval system, without the prior written permission of the copyright owner.

The moral right of the author has been asserted.

First Edition

**British Library Cataloguing-in-Publication Data.
A catalogue record for this book is available from the British Library.**

Hardback Edition ISBN 0 9530287 6 3
Paperback Edition ISBN 0 9530287 7 1

DEDICATIONS

TO

RACHEL, PANDORA AND CEDAR

as always

AND

TO

HENRY 'HARRY' ROBERT JONES, 6th Dan

Who died suddenly during the writing of this book.

We buried him in his gi.

ACKNOWLEDGEMENTS

The author and publisher would like to thank the following people for their assistance in the preparation of this book: Rachel Layton; Michael Randall, 7th Dan, Chief Instructor to the Shotokan Traditional Karate Organization (UK); Marty Randall; Nicholas Adamou, 7th Dan, Chief Instructor to the International Association of Shotokan Karate; Roger Carpenter, 6th Dan, Shotokan Karate Kanazawa-ryu International Federation; John Wise, 4th Dan, SKKIF, and Brenda Wise, 4th Dan, SKKIF; Susan Chalk, 4th Dan; Simon Bourne, 3rd Dan; Anthony Kirby, 2nd Dan, and Marcella Kirby; Vernon Bell, 9th Dan, Chief Instructor to Tenshin-Shinyo-Ryu Jujitsu (European Jujitsu Union), 3rd Dan Karate-Do, 3rd Dan Judo; Manabu Murakami, 6th Dan, SKIF; Yoko Kubokura, 2nd Dan, Master Kanazawa's personal secretary; Harry Cook, 4th Dan, Chief Instructor to the Seijinkai Karate-Do Association.

Photo credits: Hirokazu Kanazawa - 20, 21, 22, 23, 26, 34, 35, 36, 37, 40, 41, 42, 43, 44, 46, 51, 53, 55, 77, 81, 84, 86, 92, 98, 101, 102, 105, 116, 118, 119, 120, 122, 123, 126, 127, 128, 129, 130, 131, 133, 134, 135, 137, 139, 144, 145, 146, 149, 164, 165, 166, 167, 168, 170 (top), 175, 178, 180, 181; Kirby Publishing - 213; Shoto Publishing photographic library - 48, 58, 59, 60, 64, 65, 66, 67, 69, 71, 90, 94, 95, 97, 99, 106, 110, 111, 114, 121, 124, 125, 140, 170 (bottom), 186, 187.

CONTENTS

Dedications

Preface ix

I – Motivated by Revenge 19

II – Takushoku 39

III – The JKA Instructors' Course 89

IV – The JKA Championships 109

V – JKA Chief Instructor to Hawaii 143

VI – Great Britain Calling 163

References 189

Other Printed Material in English Featuring Master Kanazawa 197

Appendices 201

Glossary 207

About the Author 213

Publisher's Note 215

DISCLAIMER

The author and publisher of this book will not be held responsible in any way for any injury or damage of any nature whatsoever, which may occur to readers, or others, as a direct or indirect result of the information and instructions contained within this book.

PREFACE

Who in the world of Shotokan karate has not heard the name, Hirokazu Kanazawa? No, let me broaden that question: "Who in the world of karate, irrespective of style, has not heard of the name, Hirokazu Kanazawa?" for it is a name that has almost become synonymous with an entire art form. He is, quite simply, the most famous *karateka* alive today.

It would be sufficient to say that Master Kanazawa holds the highest black-belt rank currently bestowed by the Japanese upon any martial artist. If we then added that, despite it being true that the era of karate's popularization is now over, the master nevertheless spends at least six months of each year away from Japan, travelling the globe teaching the 2.4 million students in the one hundred and six countries that go to form the Shotokan Karate-Do International Federation, to which he is chief instructor, so that the deep spirit of karate can be imparted, it can readily be appreciated how his fame has come about. Incredibly, the SKIF is now, it is believed, operating in more countries than the Japan Karate Association.

However, Master Kanazawa's fame does not rest solely on his seniority or on the number of students within his association today, though clearly these are indicative, but on a series of contributory factors, essentially personal, but also historical, that have made the above possible. Terry O'Neill, for example, wrote in the mid 1970s that Kanazawa was "often cited by experts as the man who has come closest to achieving perfect technique ... [and that] From an aesthetic viewpoint, the karate of Kanazawa has no equal..."[1] But this technical prowess was not God-given, it was the result of a single-minded determination that has not waned in fifty years.

Another of the master's notable attributes is his ability to communicate, which may be seen as a combination of his high intelligence and the love he has for an art that he has chosen to share. Vernon Bell, the founder of British karate, reflecting back to 1965 recalled that Kanazawa's "teaching ability was so profound that even the simplest of individuals, just by copying, just by following, repeating, could feel what Kanazawa was teaching."[2] Certainly, Kanazawa always could, and still can, draw the very best from a willing pupil.

And the demonstrations! Master Kanazawa is, in the author's considered opinion, not only the finest exponent of conventional *tameshiwari* that the world of Shotokan has ever produced, but he lays claim to a strange and unique ability in the martial arts, an ability that defies the known laws of science, at least as the author understands them, in that he can reputedly board-break and brick-break selectively in a stack, with either punch or kick. Clearly, all in all, there is something very special indeed about this man.

As one might imagine, Master Kanazawa's karate lineage is of the first-order. A student, and later vice-captain of the infamous Takushoku University *dojo* for four years, he was taught by the founder of Shotokan, Gichin Funakoshi, and by Master Masatoshi Nakayama, Chief Instructor of the JKA, as well as by numerous other seniors, including Hidetaka Nishiyama and Teruyuki Okazaki. In 1956, Kanazawa was one of only three selected to enter the newly instigated one-year JKA Instructors' Course. Then, in 1957, at the first JKA All-Japan Championships, he won the individual *kumite* title despite having entered the competition with a broken hand. The following year, he won both the individual *kumite* and *kata* competitions, becoming the first JKA Grand Champion, a feat that has only been repeated five times since. In 1961 he was posted as JKA Chief Instructor to Hawaii, returning in 1963. In 1964 he studied briefly on Okinawa, and in 1965 he came to Great Britain. It is just before the trip to Europe that this book ends, for the story of 1965-1966 is told in great detail in Volume II of the author's *Shotokan Dawn*, which is currently in press, and, *The Kanazawa Years* details personal reminiscences of Michael Randall for the period 1965-1968, which covers the master's residence in Britain. Master Kanazawa then taught in West Germany for two years, acting as coach to the European team at the world championships in Mexico in 1968, before returning to Japan to take up a dual post – Principal Director of the International Section of the JKA, and as a Director of the JKA. During this time he also taught at Musashi, Kanto and Kitazato universities. He was coach to the JKA team for a number of years, and successfully took the world championship title in Paris, 1972.

In 1978, following political problems and what seems like a very acrimonious split from the then JKA, Master Kanazawa returned to Japan as a matter of honour, having originally intended to take up residence in Canada. Despite considerable family pressure to move to North America, he was determined to stay in Tokyo as the unfortunate and derogatory word *jomei* had been banded about concerning him. Alone,

PREFACE

he said he felt like a kitten compared to the might of the JKA tiger. Resolute that others were not going to determine his future, and feeling that truth would prevail and that a great test was before him, he formed SKI, essentially, from nothing. "My approach to students was to say, 'The door is open, but I'm not inviting you in. Come if *you* want to.' I never canvassed students, never poached them from other *dojo* or associations, especially not from the JKA." Class will tell, and the rest, as they say, is history – a history recorded, albeit often very sketchily, in martial arts magazines of the last twenty years or so. Since that time Master Kanazawa has spent his life teaching and building up the federation he is justly proud of, and which contains, according to the master, a staggering estimated one hundred thousand black-belts worldwide. Indeed, so great now are the numbers within SKI that a new computer system has had to be installed (away from the *dojo* because the sweat of students is affecting the workings). The greatest personal tragedy came with the premature death of his dear wife of fifteen years, Harue, aged forty-four, from cancer, in 1988. They had three sons, Nobuaki, Daizo, and Fumitoshi, all of whom attended university and all of whom have studied karate. Indeed, Nobuaki is the SKI World *Kumite* Champion, and Nobuaki and Fumitoshi met in the finals of an SKI open tournament in Japan in 1998, so the tradition continues. "Now," Master Kanazawa says, "*karateka*, all over the world, are my family." Today, he still resides in Japan, with SKI's headquarters being at 2-1-20, Minamikugahara Ota-ku, Tokyo 146-0084. His current rank of *judan* was awarded in April, 2000, while the master was attending the SKI World Championships in Bali, Indonesia. Such is his notoriety, an internationally recognizable figure, that in a number of countries, especially those with unstable political situations, the master is accorded VIP treatment, and it has not been unknown for him to have a military escort from the airport.

If one saw Master Kanazawa and had no idea of just who he was, or what he did, I believe that most observers would instinctively appreciate that here was someone of great depth and hidden strength. If one was fortunate enough to meet him socially, then one would discern a dignified, well-educated and well-mannered Japanese of good bearing, where one's initial observations of depth and strength would undoubtedly be confirmed. His posture and quietly assured composure are, without doubt, a consequence of his hard and continuous training through half a century. This practise has resulted in an astonishing physique, one that has given rise to comment by just about everyone who has seen the master in the changing room. Master Kanazawa's body is truly something to behold, an inspiration, for despite being seventy years of age, he is an anatomical chart of honed sinew and muscle that a *karateka* half his age would be proud of.

It may seem surprising then, given the remarkable nature of the man, and the seemingly endless stream of superlatives used to describe him, that no authoritative book has been written chronicling the master. Despite having being approached on a number of occasions by writers on karate and publishers around the world, the master never consented to make the time available, and all that could be gleaned had to be picked from the patchwork of material covered in interviews in martial arts magazines, and from brief biographical information from books and the master's numerous technical works, many of which have been pirated in countries where some of the populace seem to have scant regard for the notion of copyright. There was clearly a need for such a book as, *Kanazawa, 10th Dan*. In traditional karate fashion, the master wanted to entrust this form of his legacy to students he knew, and those with a proven track record. The author had known the master for twenty-six years when interviewing commenced, and the publisher of this book, Michael Randall, 7th Dan, trained with the master on the very first lesson he gave in Great Britain in April, 1965, so an atmosphere of understanding and trust was apparent throughout.

It is strange, very strange, how, just before I am about to embark on such a writing project, something extraordinary happens, involving birds, which may have an effect on how a book is written. I referred to a notable incident of this type in the preface of, *Karate Master: The Life and Times of Mitsusuke Harada*, for example, involving a wild dove. I can well understand how, in the past, from a number of diverse cultures spread through the millennia and throughout the world, birds and their flights were interpreted as portents. Within hours of meeting Master Kanazawa, a sparrowhawk flew towards me at great speed with a squealing male blackbird in its talons, and literally dropped its prey at my feet, as I stood there, mesmerized. I don't know what the ancients would have made of that, but I, of course, being the good scientist that I can be, would, no doubt, put it down to co-incidence, despite the odds, or, better still, knowing this writer particularly well, would note that if it hadn't been this incident then it would have been another; then again ...

Such was Master Kanazawa's heavy and truly exhausting schedule (he manages to continue, he says, by keeping part of his spirit from pressure), that it took over eighteen months, despite his willingness to participate in this project, to finally secure the three consecutive days necessary for the initial intensive interviewing. Roger Carpenter, 6th Dan, is to be particularly thanked for accommodating the author in this

PREFACE

regard, when three days formed a substantial percentage of the master's visit to Britain that year. The initial interviewing was conducted in the master's executive room at the Royal Adelaide Hotel, Windsor, a fine Georgian town house overlooking the notable Long Walk, an historic bridleway running from the dominating Norman Castle of William I, through to Virginia Water, a man-made lake one and a half miles in length, on the 26th-28th October, 1999, before the master flew to Brussels. Michael Randall and his student, Anthony Kirby, 2nd Dan, were in virtual continual attendance, providing all the back up one could ever ask for.

One particular interview session went on into the small hours, and I recall, on my lonely and virtually silent walk back in the fresh night air to my hotel in Eton, stopping on Windsor Bridge, gazing downstream, at first reflecting, whilst watching the glides of the Thames in the moonlight below, then slowly becoming bewitched. A mute swan swam gently out from the river bank, waking me from my dream-like state and reminding me it was time to move on, for there was more interviewing to be conducted the following morning. Down the narrow High Street every footstep echoed as I passed the Cockpit, a timber framed house dated 1420. I was based at the Christopher Hotel, an old coaching inn which, in former times, was noted as having a 'racy reputation' and, whilst strictly out-of-bounds, the irresistible charms of the establishment formed a major attraction not only to the boys of Eton College, but to their fathers alike. Both nature beyond midnight and 'houses of ill-repute' are noteworthy features in this book too.

The initial interviewing and the research that followed resulted in some forty-seven thousand words being written, but there were still uncomfortable gaps that affected the flow of the text, and it was necessary for further detailed interviewing on specific points – a battery of about one hundred and twenty questions in all. This had been predicted of course, as questions, not asked at the first meeting, naturally arose as a consequence of the writing. Thirteen months later then, on the afternoon of the 20th November, 2000, to be precise, Master Kanazawa was met from Heathrow Airport having flown in from Edinburgh. Master Manabu Murakami, 6th Dan, Chief of the International Division of SKIF, and Roger Carpenter, once again, had arranged for Master Kanazawa to stop off in London for two nights, and the final intense interviewing, commencing with a working breakfast, took place in the relaxed comfort of Tony Kirby's home in Crouch End, the whole of the following day, before the master's early morning flight to Cork, southern Ireland.

As in the case of the author's, *The Kanazawa Years,* and,

Reminiscences by Master Mitsusuke Harada, this book is a collection of recollections largely told in Master Kanazawa's own words. Whilst the format appears straightforward therefore, the manner in which the text was actually arrived at is somewhat different from that which might be readily supposed. The text is mostly a constructed monologue, a composite of the facts, figures and stories told by the master, placed in speech marks and sanctioned by him as to its content, intent and emphasis. In other words, the text is both a genuine reflection of what the master actually said, and that which he would have said if he had said it in the order presented, and with a greater command of the English language. Having made the last point however, the master was constantly referring to his Japanese/English translator, a magical little box of tricks, to ensure the author had the exact word the master wished to impart. If the book wasn't to be a biography, in the true sense of the word, which has a tendency for the creation of a distance between subject and reader, and if the flow wasn't to be interrupted by many hundreds of questions, which, scaled down, is characteristic of the usual martial arts' interview, the manner in which this work is presented was the only sensible option, and the author likes to think that the material comes over very well indeed. Sometimes, Master Kanazawa was, understandably, unsure of exact dates, and where these haven't been verified from other sources, they have been presented as believed correct by the master at the time of interviewing. Similarly, some facts and stories may be presented one or two years out of their exact temporal setting, but, once again, when covering a span of as much as seventy years, in an eventful life, this too is only to be expected. Both Master Kanazawa and the author strove for accuracy throughout, and any error is made in good faith.

On the 14th May, 2001, again at Tony Kirby's home, Masters Kanazawa and Murakami spent the whole day studiously proofing the finished manuscript, including checking photographs and their captions, and, when a few errors had been corrected, gave the book its official seal of approval, before flying back to Tokyo.

Quite naturally, some of the material contained within this work has been told before in the many brief interviews the master has given over the last thirty-eight years (the earliest referred to is 1963), usually after a training session and lasting, perhaps, an hour at most. This book brings them all together as Master Kanazawa tells them once more. Invariably, such tales are elaborated upon here. Similarly, facts about individuals, such as Gichin Funakoshi, sometimes reported elsewhere, mostly by other Japanese *karateka*, are repeated. These facts are included because Kanazawa said them and are therefore important because they provide confirmatory evidence.

Most readers will, of course, be established *karateka*, and will be familiar with most of the Japanese terms used throughout this book, for many are widely referred to in the *dojo* on a daily basis. However, a significant minority of readers will, no doubt, have only limited karate experience, and a few may have no experience at all, so for these, a two hundred and thirty-one word glossary of Japanese terms and their translations has been included at the end of the text. Providing such a glossary enabled the author to detract from placing translations in parentheses throughout the work, which can get tiresome for the reader, and when there are many such brackets, downright cumbersome, not to say irritating. All Japanese words not generally found in English concise dictionaries, excluding personal names, place names and names of martial arts, of course, are italicized for easy reference.

Throughout the interviews, Master Kanazawa referred to Japanese *karateka* without giving their first names and always ending in *sensei* (teacher) or *san* (mister), which is the Japanese custom. At the author's request, the master sought out the required first names of those unknown to the author, where possible, and these have been included in the text. These first names are only given once, and if the reader comes across a Mr. Yanase, for example, then if his first name is known, it will be found in previous text. It is the Japanese custom to give the surname followed by the first name. Throughout this work, the western custom is adhered to.

A fair number of quotations are also referred to in this book. The reader may have already noted a superscripted 1 and 2 in the third and fourth paragraphs of this preface, and there is a superscripted 3 to follow in this section. The source of these quotes is to be found in References at the end of this work. These quotes, by Master Kanazawa and others, have been included for a number of reasons, such as, the master, having referred to a particular issue in this series of interviews, has said it more pointedly in another interview; or that such quotes provide back-up information, for example, and Chapters IV and VI are particularly noteworthy in this regard with twenty-four and twenty references, respectively. There are seventy-nine references in all, though when different quotes are taken from the same reference source, whether presented in different chapters or not, the reference is repeated for reader ease in the Reference section. When text is referred to directly, the superscripted numbers are ordered numerically throughout each chapter. However, when text is not quoted, when a book is recommended for example, these superscripted numbers do not follow the ordered sequence and are placed in squared brackets. In the case of a magazine article, the reference is given in the following sequence: name of author, article title, magazine, magazine volume and/or number, and the page(s); sometimes, where possible, dates are given. For books, the sequence is: author, book title, publisher, date, and the actual page number. Quoted material often contains American English, 'practiced' as a verb, 'self-defense' with an 's', and so on, and these are included, unaltered. Following on from the references is a selected list of twenty-nine additional references, in English, that concern Master Kanazawa, that readers may wish to consult, but which were not directly referred to in the text of the present work. The range and amount of information contained within these additional references is considerable, and they have been included, chiefly, to assist future researchers.

Master Kanazawa's life may be said to fall, conveniently, into distinct episodes that have been exploited in the six chapter headings in this book. Whilst the vast majority of material forming this work is historical in nature, the master occasionally referred to contemporary SKI issues, and these have been included where they were mentioned. The latter quarter of Chapter IV is notable for a number of technical points that are raised, mostly in regard to the JKA films of the 1950s and, especially, the early 1960s, concerning changes in techniques or emphasis in *kata* movements over the years. Many readers may find some of these points concern *kata* not yet known to them, and the author would advise that whilst these points might be noted, they are not explored until the *kata* in question has been fully learned. When changes or differences occur with regard to a move within a particular form, to avoid any possible confusion, the author has referred the reader to a photograph of the movement in question in Master Kanazawa's two volume, *Shotokan Karate International Kata* books.

Kanazawa, 10th Dan was a most enjoyable book to research and write. Master Kanazawa has a wonderful sense of timing in his stories, and, especially for the humorous tales, his forceful combination of English and Japanese made the transcripting of the audio tapes truly memorable. On a number of occasions when writing this book, the tears of laughter literally ran down the author's face as he played certain stories over and over again. Of all the new tales and new facts that have come to light as a consequence of this work, and, indeed, even when taking the completed book itself into account, which, one likes to think, is well rounded (that is, there are sad stories as well, for, as Kanazawa has noted, metaphorically, he has seen the landscape of mountains and ravines), it is the master's telling of some of these humorous stories and the laughter they generated

PREFACE

that, to the author, stand out above all else. Karate-Do is a Way of life, and, as such, must reflect and balance all life's moods. If happiness can rise above sadness, when normality prevails, then surely we have chosen well.

Terry O'Neill wrote more than thirty years ago of Master Kanazawa: "He is the perfect specimen of the type of person the art of karate can develop – there will never be a finer living example of what karate at its highest level really is."[3] The present author concurs whole-heartedly with this sentiment. Kanazawa's life has been one of dedication, striving and sharing – a life where the very limits of human ability and understanding have been stretched.

May, 2001   Clive Layton, M.A., Ph.D (Lond).

KANAZAWA, 10th DAN

Calligraphy in Master Kanazawa's own hand: Kokusai Shotokan (International Shotokan)

I

MOTIVATED BY REVENGE

Hirokazu Kanazawa was born on Sunday, 3rd May 1931, in the small fishing village of Moshi, near Omoto, Iwate Prefecture, northern Honshu, the sixth of eight children, though one was adopted, to Kanbei Kanazawa and his loving and attractive wife, Masue (*née* Hatakayama), the daughter of an ironsmith, though army officers of senior rank formed part of her family background. At the time of Hirokazu's birth, his father was thirty-three years of age (born 11th December, 1897), and his mother, thirty (born 1st June, 1900). The Pacific Ocean, precipitous cliffs, and rugged mountainous backdrop, rising to some five thousand feet, dominated the lives of the twenty to twenty-five families living in Moshi, and their livelihood depended on the netting of tuna, salmon, herring, sardine, bonito, sea bream and saury pikes; from gathering shellfish and seaweed from the beach, and from farming the single summer rice crop – the winters being too cold, the snow too deep and the drainage too poor to allow for two harvests. Kanbei's father, Kansuke, had died at sea in a fearful tempest, and Kanbei, determined that he should not follow a similar fate, ran a small fleet of boats and employed local people to man them. In the 1930s, Japan was the world's foremost fishing nation supplying a staggering fifty per cent of the world's demand. Additional revenue for the Kanazawa family, in this highly competitive business, came from running a ferry from Hokkaido to the seaport of Miyako, about ten kilometres south of Omoto, primarily for the benefit of fishermen. Unfortunately, like his own father, Kanbei was not destined for a long life either. He was active in local government, and the pressures of work, coupled with the added stresses of trying to get roads and a harbour built, proved too much, and he suffered a fatal heart attack on 19th June, 1947. Masue lived for another thirty-three years, dying on the 16th December, 1980. Her life was spent devoted to her family and helping to run the family business, which is known as Kanakan.

Kanbei Kanazawa

The first child to Kanbei and Masue was a daughter, Shin (now deceased, having died of cancer after being hospitalized for one year). The second child was a son, Tetsuo, who entered and, upon his father's death, successfully took control of the family business. Yasuo was the

Masue Kanazawa – c.1920

second son, who acted as a Morse code operator, and whose hardships during the war were blamed for an early demise (of leukemia). Chuichi was the fourth child. He studied at the Marine Institute in Tokyo before and after the war, and then entered the family business before starting his own fishery firm, and died of a heart attack. The fourth son was Yusuke. He worked as a mechanic and engineer repairing the boats for the business. Later, he joined Chuichi's firm. Hirokazu followed as the

Hirokazu Kanazawa, aged seven, with his brother, Katsutomo – 1938

fifth son, and was followed in turn by an adopted boy, Katsutomo. Katsutomo was the son of Masue's brother, whose wife had died one week after giving birth. The final child, Hideo, is notable, for not only did

Masue Kanazawa with Katsutomo

he become a doctor, but he holds the esteemed rank of 8th Dan in Shotokan karate as well, being a specialist at *mae-geri* and *Sochin kata*. He studied medicine at Koryo University, but began his karate training at Takushoku University, in the open class, designed for non-Takushoku students.

The young Hirokazu was a typical cheerful boy, full of energy, and brought up under the ethics of both Buddhism and Shintoism. He studied at the Omoto Elementary School for the first six years of academic life, and then the Omoto Higher Elementary (or Junior High) for a further three years. After school, and during the holidays, he would sometimes help with Kanakan business in numerous ways – from attending the nets to assisting in the office. When not helping out, he would play football with his friends in a large garden, or sometimes on the beach, using a small ball. In the spring and summer, he would collect shellfish and seaweed from the shore, and in the autumn, berries from the hills. At Junior High School he started to learn English, and it was during this time, just after Japan had surrendered, that the young Hirokazu saw his first westerner, an American. "He was so tall, and his hair was fair. He looked so different," Kanazawa reflected. "The soldier had come to see my father in response to a request by my father for help in a search, because one of his boats had capsized and the men were missing, feared dead. My father had first visited the American office in the prefecture, much against everybody's advice. 'No. No. Don't go,' they all said. You see the Americans had just arrived and everyone was frightened of them, but my father wanted assistance in the form of an air search. He told the Japanese that the Americans would listen, for human beings are human beings, regardless of country. I think the Americans did launch a search, but the fishermen were all dead.

"Despite navigational equipment, ships would sometimes disappear without trace, as though plucked from the surface of the ocean. Kanakan ships would fish the Pacific, and then pass through the Panama Canal to exploit fish stocks in the Atlantic. Often, boats would be gone for six months. The fishermen of home were expert officers and crews and when a ship disappeared, such was the consternation and disbelief, despite the strong waves and currents in the area, that some local people offered the explanation that UFOs were to blame. Certainly, locally, to this day, the area is regarded as something of a Bermuda Triangle.

"My father was born in an age of Fascism and he strongly disapproved of that type of system. He had also had a hard life, and as a consequence became a very caring man with a pacifist philosophy. He would look after the homeless and artists who painted the sea. Often, these homeless people would stay at our house, and some were thieves. Some of them had accumulated debts, and I remember one who sold fake antique vases. My father bought such vases knowing full well that they were fakes, but he said that such people had to con in order to live.

"My father was the sort of person who realized that human beings were more important than material things. He would donate to charities and give away possessions. He would also give generously to widows with children whose husbands had been killed in wars. A friend would knock for me each morning on the way to school who had lost his father, and my father would look after him. Being brought up this way meant that the Kanazawa family's standard of living suffered considerably, but although we were poor we enjoyed ourselves and life was good.

"Sometimes, my father would come home early from work, and he would tell us stories. They were always interesting, and we would ask him to tell them over and over again, as children do.

"He would never try and impose his own ideas of what was right and what was wrong upon us. He was flexible, and I suppose he wanted us to discover what was correct for ourselves. He didn't scold us. My mother on the other hand was very strict. If you did something wrong, she would hit your back with the end of a broom, but the love was very deep within the family and there was never any real animosity. I was scolded with love.

"Talking of beatings, I remember when I was young I used to stay at my grandmother's typical small wooden house in Omoto. At her home, you could never comment as to whether you enjoyed the food or not, because she said it wasn't the taste that was important but the efforts and feelings that went into its preparation. If you left any food, you would receive a slap over the head. So, I learned to like all foods and to be thankful.

"My father loved to learn and he studied the English language quietly, by himself before the war. No one knew he understood English. Why did he do that? Perhaps he had insight? I remember when my brother, Yasuo, wrote to my father during the war. Twelve times he had been in a convoy bringing essential supplies to Japan from Taiwan, and eight times he had been sunk by torpedo. He wrote that the contest could not be won, Japan could not defeat America, the odds were simply too great. When Yasuo came home, my father said he must not write such things, for these were dangerous times. I believe my father had reasoned well in advance what the outcome of the war would be, and that was why he had learned English; so he could converse with the victors. This ability to pre-empt turned out to be important, as restrictions were placed upon the waters by the Americans as to where the Japanese could fish, and catches fell to about thirty-five per cent of their pre-war records.

"Yasuo would try and teach me English when he was on leave. He was a very clever man, very sharp. I couldn't understand, and he'd hit me. 'Are you stupid?' he'd ask. I was a healthy boy, I never became ill. Amongst Japanese country people there is a saying that only the stupid

Yasuo Kanazawa

never become ill, and so, sometimes, I felt a little ashamed. Yasuo confirmed this belief! He'd also poke me on the forehead with the blunt end of a pencil, 'Come on. Come on,' he'd say, impatiently, waiting for my answer, but I just couldn't get it. One day, he poked me much harder than usual, and the sharp end dug deep into his hand. I stifled a laugh, but I burst, and he was very angry!

"During the war, students at school were taught how to attack the enemy should an invasion take place. We practised with the wooden sword, the *bokuto*, cutting downwards, *uchi-komi*. We'd also make spears from bamboo by sharpening one end to a point. The idea was to hide in the undergrowth and when a soldier walked by, lunge out and stab him, and immediately retreat back into the forest. Normally, no one asked, but I said to my father, 'How can we fight against guns?' However, there was a philosophy that was spread at the time, that if you were not frightened of bullets, they would miss you. I never quite understood that though!

"When the men were away fighting, everybody had to do extra work. I was an eleven-year-old prefect at my elementary school, and one of the jobs we had to do was to clean a local community hall. What happened as a result of this was to affect my entire life, and provided the motivation for me to start karate. I was in-charge of a small group who regularly cleaned this hall. The next day, following such a session, I was happily walking to school with a group of my friends and a father of one of the boys in my group, a Mr. Nagayama, who I think was too old for active service, came up to me. 'You are being unkind to my son!' he shouted in a very angry tone. 'You are not treating him fairly. You are keeping him back to do extra jobs.' I didn't know what the man was talking about, because his son wasn't at school the previous day and I always considered myself fair; I prided myself on that. The man was furious and, raising his hand, he hit me with a sharp slap on the right side of my face. This was no ordinary slap however, but a full-blown *kaisho* strike. The man practised sumo, so you can imagine the effect it had on a young boy. I fell to the floor. My head was going round and round, everything was dizzy. I was completely disorientated. I couldn't see properly and I couldn't hear properly. Despite my injuries, which turned out to be serious, I thought about rugby tackling him. I didn't care if I died, as long as he died too. But I had the sense in those few short seconds to realize that I would stand no chance against this stout wrestler. I would grow stronger with the passing of time and he would grow weaker, and in the future I would fight again, pay him back for what he had done to me.

"I remember a woman passing by. She saw what had happened, and, concerned, said to the man, 'Why did you do that?' When I got to school, my teacher was very surprised at the state I was in, horrified actually. I couldn't see myself, for there were no mirrors. She sent me to the doctor immediately. He was a country doctor and I don't think he knew exactly what to do. My face swelled up so much and so quickly that when I went home, straight after attending the doctors, and stood at the door, my father, who answered it, didn't recognize me. He couldn't recognize his own son, that's how bad my injuries were. My father went to Nagayama's house and had words. 'Why have you done this to my son? Has he done something very bad?' my father demanded. Nagayama replied that I had kept his son back very late on numerous occasions and that the boy was being unfairly treated by me. The man admitted that he had acted rashly, and paid my father considerable compensation. Eventually the truth came out. The boy went to his father and confessed that he had come home late because he had been out playing, and that he'd used me as an excuse. He had lied. His father said that it was too late; the damage had been done.

"After this incident, my studies went downhill very quickly. My eyes became weak, I couldn't concentrate, and bones in the inner ear had been broken and the eardrum shattered. I was deaf in the right ear an instant after the *kaisho* had made contact. There was nothing that anyone could do. I could hear noises in my head like radio interference, and I could not concentrate for periods exceeding half an hour. I'd bang my head to try and get rid of the noises. They were a dreadful torment. Not long ago I saw a specialist again, and he said that it was inoperable. I've seen two specialists, one in Japan and another in Mexico. My eyes became stronger with special exercises. I had a love of mathematics and was very quick at calculating, but the noises in my head were an unrelenting distraction and I found that I could no longer enjoy something that had given me pleasure and that I had been good at. I was determined to get even with Nagayama for what he'd done to me, and revenge provided the sole motivation in my life for the next ten years.

"It was at this time that I began my love of astronomy. In the evenings, for two hours, eight until ten, or sometimes nine until eleven, I would go outside and watch the heavens, count the number of shooting stars, that kind of thing. Away from pollution, the skies were clear and beautiful. I found it very relaxing, very peaceful, and, strangely, the noises in my head would stop. I didn't have any optical equipment; I just used to watch the heavens. My father was interested in the stars for navigational purposes, and so was Katsutomo. Now I have a powerful reflecting telescope at my home, very expensive. I don't have many astronomy books, but those that I have are well thumbed, as I used to read them on plane journeys. I have no special interests within astronomy, I simply like to watch and wonder at the universe, the gas clouds, the life of stars, galaxies, black holes, and to let my mind roam free in the vastness of space. I find it gives me a lovely feeling of harmony, and my problems disappear. I came to realize that 'the [human] body is the same as the universe; each body is a small universe. All things are related and you must remember this when training in karate.'[1]

"I also liked to walk along the pebble beach, beachcombing. I found that very simple, childlike and contemplative. The cliffs are steep at Omoto and there are stacks not far from the beach, the softer intervening rock having been eroded away, thus the stacks have become detached from the mainland. Sometimes I would go for a swim in the sea, but I had to be careful, for it is a wild area. Iwate Prefecture is known as the Tibet of Japan.

"Another pastime, which actually turned out to be more than just a pastime, that I liked to do, was night fishing. After school, a friend, or brother, and I, would walk down to the nearby beach and perch ourselves, sometimes precariously, on rocks over deep pools. We only used bamboo rods, line and large baited hooks; nothing sophisticated. As the light faded and evening came on, we would fish these pools feeling the line. One began to learn the movement and rhythm of the waves and the shifting currents through the line and through the tips of the fingers, despite moving the bait, encouraging the fish, as we were, to bite. In the pitch dark, with the sound of the waves crashing against the rocks, this form of fishing proved to be a wonderful form of natural concentration. In spite of all the distractions on the senses, and all the 'interference' on the line, I found I could feel a fish investigating my bait, playing with it, deciding whether to take it or not. In this way, I came to learn the mind of a fish, and I felt I knew what they were going to do, though not always! I believe this night fishing helped me in my later practice of karate, gave me something that's difficult to explain, a kind of tuning. I found that karate allowed me to build upon this sensitivity, and I could feel what an opponent was going to do. This ability is now usually dormant in man, but hard karate practice can sensitize you to it, and enhance its development.

"I also tried my hand at calligraphy, but found it extremely demanding, and I didn't seem to improve. I also liked to read biographies, of which that of Nishyo Inue stands out in my mind. I practised the Japanese flute, *shakuhachi*, but it is an incredibly difficult instrument to learn. It takes three years training before the right sound comes. It is very good training for the *hara* and I'd like to go back to practising it, especially now that I have stopped playing golf. The reason why I stopped playing golf is because in Japan a round is twenty-seven holes, and you start early in the morning and continue into the evening. I simply do not have the time for that. Yes, I shall buy a *shakuhachi*.

"I have also started to study *Iaido*. I practise downward cuts against straw. It is very difficult to cut properly, a very precise art. In the beginning, I would hit the wet straw at the wrong angle and I broke five swords, as they would wedge. It was very expensive training! Now, I cut cleanly. I practise at a friend's house, a farmer, in the country. Today, if I am challenged by a *kendoka*, I will not worry. Such practice is very good for confidence. It is also very good for the hips, *hara* and *kiai*. The sword action must be smooth and you cut through. It is important not to focus one's attention on the point of incision, but on the point of exit. Studying *Iaido* is very good for teaching mind set. You cut like a shooting star. This is not karate *ki*, but Chinese *chi*; they are different.

"It took many, many months for my face to go back to normal. As soon as I was able, I undertook the process of calculated revenge. I wanted a martial arts teacher, but there weren't any where I lived, so I began improvising, doing what an eleven year old could do. I started punching and kicking heavy, thick hemp ropes in the Kanakan stock room. I'd wrap towels around my fists and punch as hard as I could. I started running in the mountains for fitness and to build a strong spirit. My parents just thought I was getting strong and healthy, they didn't know what I had in mind.

"All four of my elder brothers practised a martial art and I learned what I could from them. Tetsuo was a notable *judoka*, receiving his *Shodan* at Junior High School, and he taught me judo. Later, when I went to High School, through his influence I was able to practise at the local police *dojo*, and this was good training. This was when the American occupying forces banned the martial arts. Only the police were allowed to train in judo, so I was very lucky. Yasuo studied judo and sumo, and Chuichi, judo and kendo. Yusuke studied judo and boxing. My younger brother, Katsutomo, although small, played rugby. He was a very fast runner, and when we fought, I could never catch him. Hideo was younger still, but did not influence my martial arts because of his age. My father was tall, nearing six feet, and very strong, though he never practised a martial art. Once a famous *judoka* came to our village, but he couldn't throw my father. My father didn't practice, but he couldn't be thrown by a master ... 'Ah! Something to learn,' I thought. Yes, I remember that incident well.

"My uncle, my father's younger brother, was a very famous master of Shin-koku-ryu, a system of jujitsu or *yawara* as we used to say.

Later, I watched him practise *kata* that contained many feints, like slapping the legs and moving the legs without real intent, just like some of the moves in *Gankaku-sho*. I learned to punch and kick from him. Off I'd go to the top of the family business building in Miyako, which could sleep thirty men, and practise my techniques, still striking ropes and nets, and always thinking of Nagayama.

"My brother, Chuichi, when at school, had a classmate whose name was Yamashiro. He was Okinawan and was a student in Tokyo. Every holiday, spring, summer and winter, he'd come to Omoto and Miyako and work for my father and earn some money. He studied karate and, despite being only nineteen or twenty when I first saw him, had excellent physical ability. He would train alone in the open air, and would stop if he saw anyone watching. I was about fourteen or fifteen when I met him and I would crouch or lie down in the undergrowth and watch him practise *kata*. I don't know what style it was, but it was very impressive. I watched him for three years when I was at Junior High School and then High School. The school system has changed now.

"I was with my friends one day, and I remember asking Yamashiro if he would break a rock for us. We went down to the beach and collected a large rock, and brought it back to him. Bang! He broke it! My friends and I were really impressed. It was just so exciting for impressionable young boys. Yamashiro was very, very strong. He'd also break bamboo, just above the knot, with *shuto*. I recall that he also broke glass with *uraken*, without ever being cut; he was that fast and that accurate. I would never advise anyone to try that though. Of course, as boys, we were tempted to emulate Yamashiro, but common sense prevailed thank goodness. Get it wrong and you can cut your wrist and bleed to death.

"One day Yamashiro got drunk and the proprietor of the establishment telephoned the police. A large and well known policeman named Kodama, who was a 5th Dan in judo, and much respected – even the local *yakuza* wouldn't meddle with him – tried to sort things out, but Yamashiro jumped up and, with an *uraken*, broke Kodama's nose. The other policemen jumped on him and took him to the station. Chuichi went along to the police station the next day and bailed him out. Yamashiro was a role model for me, and the main inspiration why I later studied karate and not another martial art. No one thought that Kodama could be beaten, and yet Yamashiro did it with apparent ease. You must also understand that karate was Okinawan, and hardly anyone had heard of it in Japan, especially in the rural parts. It was mysterious, and the movements were not Japanese.

"When I was eighteen and at High School, I studied boxing, European boxing. I studied privately at a temple. At school I played rugby, but every day I practised judo, secretly. The school went on a field trip to Tokyo, and I had the opportunity to watch Yoshio Shirai, who became Japan's first world boxing champion. [Shirai out-pointed Hawaiian, Dado Marino, in Tokyo in 1952, to take the World Flyweight title – the same year the Japanese Boxing Commission was established. Shirai, who was 5′5", held the title for two years before being out-pointed after fifteen rounds by the diminutive (4′10$^{1}/_{2}$") and legendary Argentinian, Pascual Perez, in Tokyo, in November 1954. Perez, who had previously drawn with Shirai over ten rounds in Buenos Aires in July that year, went on to hold the title until 1960]. Shirai was with an American academic, a Dr. Kahn, who was a scientist, a Ph.D. In those days boxers tended to slog it out, but Kahn was interested in avoidance strategies, then in, bang!

"One night my youngest brother, Hideo, was sleeping in my parents' bed. My mother heard my father give a strange exhalation, primaeval. My father had suffered a coronary in his sleep. We called an uncle round urgently, but he couldn't revive my father, and so that's how he died. His premature death came as a very great shock to the family, because it wasn't suspected for a moment. I suppose I was in mourning for a year, but you never get over something like that, and it still comes back to me. To make matters worse, the day before he died I was in the warehouse punching and kicking the ropes and he called out for me. I looked through a crack in the wood, but didn't answer him, as I thought I might be in trouble. That was the last time I heard my father, and I will always wonder what it was that he wanted to say. It is not a nice thing to live with, as it can play on your mind.

"I will remember my father as someone who was always smiling, who was kind and never shouted. I recall once, when I was very young, I went into a shop and picked up some shirts. I wasn't old enough to understand about money, and I thought that you could just help yourself and that the shirts were free. My father must have paid for them, but he never said anything to me about the cost, nor about the fact that we didn't need shirts, nor about how hard he had to work to earn the money to support the family. He just loved all his children. He was held in high regard by the community, and was a supporter of Zenko Suzuki, who later became Prime Minister [in 1980. In 1947, at the age of thirty-six, Suzuki was elected to the lower house of the Diet as a Socialist party deputy. Previously, he had studied at the Academy of Fisheries during the 1930s]. My father was once asked to run for parliament, but he refused, as he did not believe that a politician should have business interests.

"My father's death brought a great responsibility for Tatsuo, as he had to take over the family's concerns, as he became responsible for the developing family. He was only twenty-seven at the time, and had to grow up fast, too fast. My mother was hard with Tatsuo; I suppose she had to be. She kept strong for the family, and I never really knew, I don't think any of us really knew, how she felt about her husband's death. She kept it all very much to herself.

"It was decided that it would be best if not all the members of the family studied fishery, and so I enrolled at the Iwaizumi Agricultural High School and stayed there one year. All the young students came from farming backgrounds and were already very good at handling cows, pigs and other animals. I had no idea and I think the animals sensed this. The cows and horses wouldn't respond to me at all. The academic side was no problem, but the practical side for me was very difficult. At harvesting, we were set a task, using the scythe let's say, and after two or three hours the other students had finished. They went home, and I was barely half finished. I was very unhappy and always behind. I saw no way of ever catching up, and as the course progressed I was being left further and further behind and there was nothing I could do about it, as I could not gain the experience in the allotted time. Normally, when you use agricultural implements, you get calluses on your hands, but I got growths instead, and damaged my hands. I had to have an operation on my right hand below my second finger. I got very down. I got depressed. I began to get a complex, to question my abilities and self-worth. My self-esteem had plummeted. I had to be realistic, so I left and went into something I knew all about, something I should have done from the start, fishery management. I had, in a sense, wasted a year though, for I had to start in Year 1 of the fishery school. Normally, one attended High School for three years, but I stayed four years.

"When I was at Agricultural High School, funny things happened to me as well. I remember a senior, a prefect in the year above, came up to me and gave me a piece of paper and said I had to get what was written down. I read it, but I didn't understand it. I was living at my uncle's home, a traditional Japanese wooden house, in Iwaizumi, and he had four daughters. I showed them the paper, but they didn't understand it either. The only word we could understand was pharmacist, so one of the daughters, who was about ten years old, took it to the local pharmacy, and I gave the girl a few coins to buy a treat. I then gave the sealed package to the senior. The pharmacist came to see my uncle and said, 'You shouldn't send one of your young daughters to get condoms for you!' My cousin told him who had sent her to the pharmacist and my

Master Kanazawa off to Fishery High School – 1949

uncle was angry with me. It is funny now, but it wasn't so funny then.

"The next day, I went back to the prefect and asked him why he had done this to me, why he had embarrassed me this way. Then, suddenly, Bang! He slapped the side of my face. I just stood there. 'One!' I counted, indignantly. Then he hit me on the other side of the face. 'Two,' I counted. After seven slaps he stopped and walked away. Shortly afterwards, I went to where he lived and challenged him to a fight. He was bigger than me and he had confidence, but it was a matter of honour, a matter of pride. We fought for thirty minutes, punching, kicking, grappling,

Master Kanazawa at the time of his entry into High School

and I knocked him out and went home. The incident was reported to the police by the woman who owned the house this senior was lodging at, and the next day I was called in to see the Headmaster. He wanted to

Members of the rugby class, High School, 1950. Sitting, on the left, is Nakaya, and in front, Kobayashi.

expel me, but he had to do it diplomatically, because my father was an influential man, and so it was decided that I would stay at the Agricultural School until the end of the year. And that's another reason why I went

Tetsuo Kanazawa with Esu

to Fishery School! Usually, an incident like this would have put an end to any more study.

"I also recall looking after a consignment of my family's fish at the docks, making sure that no one stole them. The fish would be unloaded and then bought by another company. It was a fish market. Two seniors from the fishery school were damaging the fish and I asked them to stop. 'This is for people to eat,' I said, 'Please do not touch.' One of them, out of the blue, hit me on the right side of the face, just where Nagayama had. It wasn't so hard, but I didn't need it, and it made me very uncomfortable. I didn't fight back this time because I was in the employment of my father as it were, and I didn't want to give him a bad name. After I had completed my watch, I went back to my father's office, a little down-hearted. They asked me what had happened. My face must have still been red. Now, my father employed many strong people, *judoka* of 4th Dan and 5th Dan, *kendoka*, sumo wrestlers, and they went to see the boy responsible. They told him not to hit the son of the boss, or else. I never got bothered again.

"During the holidays when I was at High School, I'd travel back to Omoto. Mister Nagayama knew I would be back; it was just a question of when. He'd leave his house early in the morning and would go into the mountains to work and to hide and would not come back until late in the evening. He knew I was after him. One day, when I was in my first or second year at High School, so it was some years after I'd been struck, I returned home during one spring or summer vacation. I was out in the surrounding countryside with the family Alsatian, whose name was Esu, and I came across Nagayama walking with his wife. The dog was on the lead, and when he saw Nagayama he really wanted to attack him. I don't know how the dog could have known; it's very strange, a sixth sense. I was happy that Esu could understand my history without the need for language. I had to hold the lead firmly and had quite a bit of trouble restraining him to be honest, despite being, virtually, my current size. If I'd let Esu off the lead, I think he may have killed Nagayama. Nagayama was petrified, for there was nowhere he could run to, and he thought I was going to let the dog off. But I didn't release Esu because of the man's wife. I had no intention of harming an innocent party. I knew my time would come to get even, especially as I now knew his time and route. He must have taken every precaution to avoid me however, for even though I would often lay in wait for him at different locations and at different times along the trail, he never used that route again."

II

TAKUSHOKU

Just short of his twentieth year, the young Kanazawa travelled, by rail, the five hundred or so kilometres south to Tokyo. The capital was a sprawling metropolis of nearly seven million people, the largest city in the world, huge numbers of evacuees having returned following the mass exodus to the countryside caused by the American bombing.

Master Kanazawa continued: "Before I went to Takushoku University [the master often referred to Takudai, which is the familiar name for the same institution], I had one year at Nippon University, that would be 1951-1952, reading marine studies – fishery management, oceanography, and so on. I was now intending to enter the family business and was studying specifically for that. It was a private university and my family paid about two thousand pounds Sterling a year, by today's standards, to send me there. The fees for the course were not that bad, but Tokyo was very expensive, and with lodging, food, books, and so on, it was a lot for my eldest brother, now in-charge of the family funds, to find. During this year I spent my time looking for the right type of karate *dojo*, and I visited many universities apart from Nippon, such as Keio, Chuo, Waseda, Senshu, Hosei and Takushoku. I didn't know about different styles, and I just went to observe.

"There were Wado-ryu and Goju-ryu clubs at Nippon, but the Shotokan club had just started up that year and they were all beginners. I had a few lessons, but there was no history, no heritage, and I didn't like it at all. The club didn't even have a *dojo*, and we practised in a normal study room after putting the tables and chairs to the sides. The karate was not what I had imagined; I needed to find what my mind wanted. I tried the judo as well, but I didn't like that either.

"The karate that really stood out for me was that practised at Takushoku. Oh! This I liked. I was greatly impressed. My first glimpse of it was through a gap in the wooden *dojo* wall, when I was outside. I saw Mr. Teruyuki Okazaki, Mr. Hidezo Kurosawa, Mr. Tunejiro Minoda

Master Kanazawa and Yamashiro by the statue of Takamori Saigo in Ueno Park, Tokyo. Master Kanazawa was about to sit the entrance examination for Nippon University – March, 1951.

and Mr. Takamichi Arai. They all looked very strong, and so fast. Yes, I liked this very much. This was my idea of karate at the time. I wanted to do it whatever the sacrifice.

"Some of the karate sparring at other universities, especially the Goju-

Master Kanazawa as a student of Nippon University – 1951

ryu, was very close, but I preferred distance – I felt it suited my build, and I also like the wider, longer stances of Shotokan. You may remember that I practised boxing, and I had a false confidence. I thought I could look after myself. I was a young man; I had a big head. I had heard that

Master Kanazawa with brothers Hideo (sitting) and Katsutomo – 1951

it could be dangerous if members of a karate club thought you were a student from another university, so, when I was questioned, I said that I was from Meijin High School. This way, they thought that I might want to join their karate club next year. I was a prospective candidate you might say. I had confidence, but I also used strategy.

A student of Nippon University with a former classmate from High School – 1951.

"I asked my professor at Nippon, Saburo Kawada, if I could apply for a one-year credit transfer from Nippon to Takushoku, and he said no. The professor was my brother's senior – they had both attended the

Master Kanazawa as a student of Nippon University – 1951

fishery university in Kanagawa – and I entered Nippon through the recommendation of this professor. So, I left, and was resolved to start again, as I had done at High School. I secretly took the examination for Takushoku and passed, and then began lectures without telling my family what I'd done.

"The philosophy of Takushoku was one that I liked – to spread out, to help others, to aid development, to improve culture, to give and recognize independence ['Takushoku literally means cultivation and colonization'¹]. It was like my father having faith that the Americans would help their fellow man, despite being former enemies, and the fact that the Americans did help. Takushoku was founded in 1900, and started as a Taiwan school, not Japanese. The spirit of the university is made clear in the university song, part of which says that Budo is all that is left. Takushoku is only about two kilometres from where the old Shotokan *dojo* used to stand. The fees for Takushoku were a little less than for Nippon, and whereas at Nippon there were many departments, Takushoku specialized in political economy and commercial science. In those days there were only the two departments, but nowadays there are many subject areas offered, with diverse courses available. Political economy tended to be more theoretical, whereas commerce was more business orientated, more practical, if I can make that crude distinction. Anyway, many karate students found that because of their karate commitments their academic studies suffered.

"After enrolling for my bachelor's degree in commerce in 1952, the new undergraduates were asked to make a line and were then quizzed by seniors as to what sports or arts they had studied at High School, what their interests were, and so on. I replied that I had played rugby. I had chosen Takushoku solely with karate in mind, so I wasn't going to say anything about judo. 'But haven't you done some judo?' they enquired. I couldn't lie, so I replied that I had done a little, which wasn't true, as I had reached 2nd Dan. They said that if I had trained in judo, even for a short time, I should continue. I said, 'No! I want to study karate.' I was adamant. I told them that I had joined Takushoku specifically to practise karate, but they insisted I practise judo. I was very unhappy, as you can imagine. I got a letter from the judo captain asking me to bring my futon to the judo dormitory. I couldn't enrol for karate because I was worried about what the judo captain might do if I disobeyed.

"Later, I signed up for the karate, and the judo captain heard about it. I was training in basics, '*ichi, ni, san*,' and I looked up and saw the judo captain standing at the *dojo* entrance with his arms folded. He was just staring at me, not taking his eyes off me. I was very frightened. I had disobeyed my senior, and in the Japanese university system of that time, you just didn't do that. Every day for a week he came into the *dojo*, and just stood there with his arms folded, watching me. I didn't know what he was going to do. But I thought that if he hit me, he wouldn't kill me, so I carried on training. At the end of the week he called me over. I was really worried, seriously worried. 'Perhaps today I will get my beating,' I thought. He said that I'd worked really hard in the karate lessons and that I obviously liked it and was suited to it, so I had better train in karate. But, he added, I must train hard and not give up. He was a fair man. It was such a relief. I was so happy.

"It was the custom at Takushoku karate club, which was formed in 1933, for all beginners to shave their heads after enrolling. Well, I say shave, I suppose an extreme crew cut would best describe it. Because I had started late however, I never complied with this tradition and it was overlooked. I never wanted to shave my head at the time in any case. The heads were shaved only the once.

"After two months training, a taxi unexpectedly arrived outside my lodgings, and two of my karate classmates got out. They said I had to go with them, and asked me to pack my clothes and belongings, for I had been chosen to live in the karate dormitory. I said I couldn't go just like

Master Kanazawa at the time of his entry into Takushoku University

that, my family had to be informed. My eldest brother needed to be consulted, for he had sorted out my lodgings, and so on. The classmates wouldn't take no for an answer though, they insisted, and I had to pack my bags. From that time on I was to be an inside student, which was a privilege, but also very hard. There were only five of us in my dormitory, and the room was so small, smaller than a hotel bedroom, so things were really cramped. I lived like this for four years. There were a total of twenty karate students living-in at Takushoku at the time, and they were mostly brown or black-belts. I was a white-belt of course, so they must have seen something in me." [Master Kanazawa was reluctant to admit that he had been chosen because of the spirit he had shown in his training and for the underlying talent the seniors obviously spotted, but intimated that that was why he had been asked to lodge at the university]. Master Okazaki, noted: 'All of the team members were required to live in a dormitory provided by the university so we could train together day and night.'²

Master Kanazawa continued: "At my first year at Takushoku, Mr. Okazaki, who was a 2nd Dan at the time I think, was the captain of the karate club, an important position, and Mr. Toshio Irie and Mr. Onoue were the vice-captains. They were strong *karateka*, really very strong, dynamic. Okazaki was a clever person, a gentleman. His technique was very correct, perfect, especially his kicks – his side-kicks were wonderful. Mister Irie liked sparring. Mister Onoue was taller and gentle, and he was kind to the juniors.

"As I say, I hadn't told my family that I'd changed universities. I knew they would be upset, so I just kept quiet about it. At the end of my first year at Takushoku however, the bill for the fees to Nippon came to the family home. My mother gave me the money, but instead I paid my Takushoku University fees with it. Then, shortly afterwards, there was a karate demonstration in Tokyo with all styles coming together, and with Funakoshi *Sensei* in attendance. A reporter and photographer from a national newspaper, *Maimichi Shimbun*, one of three papers to be distributed throughout Japan, came down to cover the event. The reporter did quite a write-up and there was a picture of me performing a jump-kick, a *tobi-geri*, as a brown-belt on Mr. Sata, a fellow student, under which was written, 'Takushoku student – Kanazawa, Hirokazu.' Many people in Omoto read the paper and were very surprised. They went to my home in Moshi and congratulated my mother on her son being featured. My mother, of course, thought that I was attending Nippon. 'No! No!' she said to them, 'It cannot be the same person.' Then someone showed her the newspaper, 'Look, here he is,' they answered, and handed it to her. 'No!' my mother exclaimed, 'Kanazawa is not an uncommon name. It must be someone else who looks very similar.' 'Oh!' the other person replied, 'Look, the first name is Hirokazu!' I received a telephone

Master Teruyuki Okazaki

call from home. My secret was out! I had to go back to Moshi to explain myself, to apologize. Initially, only Yasuo, who was hospitalized at this time, supported me. He liked the martial arts and was on my side. Tatsuo said it was too late to argue the point as I had started the new course at the new university. My family rallied round me, but placed the responsibility on my head that I must try to be the number one *karateka* in Japan. 'I will try,' I said, 'I promise I will try.'

"The initial karate training at Takushoku was mostly in basics. Every single day we had to face the *makiwara*, which were located just outside the *dojo*. I think there were about fifteen of them, embedded in the ground, in a line. Some universities, such as Waseda, had *makiwara* inside as well. There was no escaping the *makiwara*. On each occasion we'd punch the *makiwara* a minimum of two hundred times each hand, *gyaku-zuki*, and perform one hundred *haito*, one hundred *uraken*, and one hundred *shuto*, each hand, and also, *chudan-mawashi-empi*. We'd kick one hundred times each leg with *mawashi-geri*, *kekomi* and *ushiro-geri*. For *mae-geri* we'd mostly practise on the large sandbag that hung in the *dojo*. We also practised the other types of kick on the bag. We'd train in *keage* on the bag, kicking upwards, and making contact with the underside of the bag.

"When I started punching on the straw pads of the *makiwara*, the skin broke, which is normal, but because of the daily pounding, severe training, the grazes got worse and worse, and became deep, bloody crevices. On one occasion I recall pulling straw from such a crevice and quite clearly seeing the bone underneath. We used to put iodine on these very deep cuts – Ah! The pain! Every day we used to do this. The seniors said that it was spirit training. One day, I went to the hospital for another reason, and when the doctor saw the state of my hands he informed me that it was extremely dangerous. He advised me to stop immediately, and told me such practice would cause irreparable damage, and that a really bad infection could set in that might well work its way up the arm. I went back to the *dojo* all bandaged up. 'No!' the seniors said, and they ordered me to take the bandages off and started me punching the *makiwara* forthwith. The pain – it was absolute hell!"

Concerning *makiwara* training at Takushoku, Master Shiro Asano – now an 8th Dan residing in Nottingham, England – who attended the karate club a few years later, noted: "At Takushoku we could not stop. We had to carry on whatever the injury. There was not much concern for health and there was a lot of infection through cuts."[3]

There was nothing new in this type of training, for Master Funakoshi commented on the subject nine years before, when Japan was at war. He wrote: "Swollen fists can be soaked in cold water to ease the pain and make the swelling subside, but if you break the skin, you won't be able to use the *makiwara* for a week or two. There are, of course, those stout-hearted high school and college students who, hating to lose, ignore abraded skin, grit their teeth, and go on striking the straw pad until it is dyed deep red with their blood. Their spirit is admirable, but they can't help throwing weaker and weaker punches. In the end there is not much benefit."[4] Likewise, in his autobiography [5] of 1956, he repeated the advice. However, as Master Kanazawa noted, "The Takushoku seniors had their own ideas," and these clearly did not take into account the founder's concerns that "over-training can not only injure the knuckles, sometimes permanently, but it may occasionally be the cause of diseases of the internal organs."[6]

Master Kanazawa continued: "The karate *dojo* was small, and measured only about ten metres by six metres. You could get about thirty people in there. It had old style windows, no glass, just wooden shutters, that opened sidewards. In my third year, we moved to a new *dojo*, which was bigger. You could get fifty students in there without any problem. There were windows on one side and old-style shutters on the other side. Both *dojo* had wooden floors and wooden walls, and were used solely for karate, every day. Whilst the new *dojo* had space, I actually preferred the old one, because with a small space there was no escape; you had to learn to defend yourself, you couldn't keep stepping back. The old *dojo* bred strength.

"The training in the *dojo* was officially conducted six days a week, but something invariably happened on the Sunday, and so we never had a rest. Because I had started late as a student at the club, I decided to practise by myself, at night. I reasoned that I had to train more than my classmates, otherwise I'd always be behind. The dormitory was adjacent to the *dojo*, and every night, past midnight, and being careful not to wake my seniors, I crept downstairs and turned right into the *dojo*. I couldn't put the lights on of course for fear of waking others, so I learned to find my way in the pitch dark using a mental image. This was very good training in a number of ways.

"I didn't have to go outside, the dormitory and *dojo* were joined. When I got inside, I trained in the dark. Sometimes the light of the moon would shine through the shutters and provide me with some reference points. One moonless night, I came to the *dojo* entrance and there, before me, was an apparition, a ghost. We had been told a story by the seniors, that some years before a student had hung himself in the *dojo* because he had found the training too hard. Of course, this tale came immediately to mind, as I saw this strange, faint, slow moving image before me.

"My first reaction was naturally to escape and I turn away, but my

On the occasion of welcoming new members to Takushoku – 1952. Master Kanazawa's companion is Fujito.

legs wouldn't respond. I was that terrified. Then the thought came to me, 'Why do I train in karate? I must not be frightened!' So, I turned back to face the spectre, which was about ten metres away, at the far end of the *dojo*. Very slowly, very cautiously, my heart pounding, I walked towards the shimmering image. I could still not make sense of it. It looked human, but I wasn't sure. Then, out of the darkness came a sharp, 'Kanazawa!' and I almost jumped out of my skin. It turned out to be a classmate, Tamotsu Terada. Only he and I were complete beginners at the Takushoku karate club, our classmates having studied karate at High School, and he had had the same idea as me, but he trained in front of a mirror with a faint candle to the side, and it was his strange and distorted image reflected in the dimmest of lights that I had mistaken for the ghost. Not long after, I really did see a ghost, twice [see later in this chapter].

"Terada explained that he trained every night, and when I said that I did also, I enquired why I hadn't seen him before. It turned out that Terada had crept into the *dojo* and heard someone, me, training in the darkness, and had gone away and returned after I had finished, normally about 2.00 am. I trained more for form and movement, *kihon* and *kata*, and I would also practise *kumite* by myself, and imagine a partner out of the blackness. I especially liked kicking techniques, all kicks, I had no favourite, and I would practise these too. As a child, at elementary school, I used to pick stones up with my toes and skim them across the water to see how many skips they would make before they sank. I used to do this using a *mawashi-geri*-type technique and, later, a *mae-geri*-type technique. My toes became very agile and responsive, like fingers.

"I became quite well known in Omoto for my dexterity. One of my favourite pastimes, when wearing wooden *geta*, was to entertain the fishermen. I'd perform a *mawashi-geri*-type kick and aim the *geta*. It would fly off my foot at great speed and hit the target. I never had any trouble from the fishermen!

"At Takushoku, I could easily take a person's cap off with *mawashi-geri*, keeping the peak held between my toes, and then replace the cap with *gyaku-mawashi-geri* – hat off, hat on, just like that. I used to do the same thing with cigarettes – take them out of people's mouths, and then put them back. I was very adept with my feet and legs.

"Terada, on the other hand, at night, trained more for eyes and speed. From then on, we continued training separately, but sometimes practised together as well.

"Not only was the training at Takushoku very demanding, but so was the daily schedule. In my first year, because I was the dormitory junior, I had to get up every morning before my seniors. I would rise at 6.00 am and clean the *dojo* and changing rooms, which had to be kept spotless. Sometimes, a senior would come in and inspect, looking for dust, just like a sergeant. From 6.30 am until 7.30 am we had karate practice. Breakfast

A group photograph of Takushoku University karate students on Oshima Island, one full day's trip by boat from Tokyo. It was a training exercise – climbing the volcano, with its difficult, sharp-rocked terrain, in *geta*. Master Kanazawa can be seen, second from right, back row, standing on solidified lava – 1952.

was served at 8.00 am. At 9.00am university classes began, and these continued until 3.00 pm. At 3.30 pm we had another two hours karate, and I had to clean the *dojo* again. Every time the *dojo* was used, it had to be cleaned. I cleaned the *dojo* every day during my first year. Dinner was at 6.30 pm, and then we had further academic studies. When I had to prepare the meals – breakfast, lunch and dinner – which were organized on a rota basis with the dormitory *kyohai*, I had to miss training. This happened, I suppose, once, sometimes twice a week. These breaks were very welcome – no need to train today! On Tuesday and Thursday evenings there was special additional training with the seniors. These were gruelling classes. At 10.30 pm it was bed. However, it was only rest for me if my seniors were in bed, otherwise I'd have to wait for them. It was very hard. In the years that followed, everything remained much the same, except that I didn't have to prepare the meals.

"The food was very simple – soup, a few pickles, a few vegetables – but rice was expensive. We sometimes had to 'borrow' some vegetables from local allotments. We had no money. Very occasionally we'd get some small fish or meat to put into the soup, or serve them with the rice. The juniors were so hungry that we'd boil the meat in the soup for an hour and eat a bit here and eat a bit there as the preparation went on. I remember on one occasion I served Mr. Okazaki, and after a short while he called me back. 'Kanazawa!' he said. '*Oss!*' I shouted, and went running. 'This soup smells very nice,' he continued, 'It smells of meat, a good meat smell. But I cannot find the meat?' '*Oss!*' I replied, feigning a puzzled expression, 'What has happened?' Of course we'd eaten it all during the preparation.

"Two students were assigned to meals and we worked together in a small kitchen that had been specially built. The kitchen had a wood burner, but cut-up wood was expensive, and any money went on food, so we'd find an old derelict house, not too uncommon after the war, and chop wood up. Sometimes, we'd go to a cemetery and collect wood. We'd take the pieces of wood with writing on them, prayers for the dead. We'd offer a short prayer in turn, 'Sorry! Sorry! Very sorry!' we'd say, 'but our need is very great and we are living!'

"Students would come to Takushoku and the other Tokyo universities from all over Japan, from Okinawa to Hokkaido. What wasn't always appreciated was that tastes differed considerably according to where you had been brought up. In Iwate Prefecture, one of the usual meals was *nattou*, it comes from beans, and I think you call it bean curd. I thought everyone in Japan ate it, and I made it often, because it is cheap, but I found that the people from Kyushu, south Japan, never ate it and didn't like it at all.

"Our diet was very poor and this had an effect upon me. Of course, when you are training as hard as we were, you needed a normal diet plus a bit extra. I wasn't getting enough even for a normal person. I thought every one was enduring this food and surviving, so I had to as well. I could have asked for more money from my family so that I could eat out, but I didn't want to. I wanted to do what I believed the other dormitory students were doing. One day, I hit my leg on the reflex point below the knee, and nothing happened. I pulled my skin and the elasticity in the skin seemed to have gone, like an old person's skin. I would pinch and pull the skin and it wouldn't go back. It turned out that I was suffering from malnutrition. I didn't have an ounce of fat on me when I began training because I was in good condition, and I couldn't afford to lose an ounce, but I lost about one quarter of my body weight I suppose. The doctor was surprised at my condition. I also had a calcium deficiency. Before I went to university I had very good teeth, but they went bad. My brother was worried and got me some vitamin tablets, and I had to take one tablet twice every day, morning and evening. I then found out that everyone, all the dormitory people, were eating outside.

Due to the large initial intake into the Takushoku karate club, training had to be conducted outside. The karate *dojo* is out of picture, but is immediately in the direction that the students, practising *Heian Yondan*, are looking towards – 1953.

"At the beginning of each academic year, there was an influx of new students. At Takushoku there would be one hundred *karateka* each April. The old *dojo* wasn't really large enough to cope with a third of that number and we had to train outside in the university grounds. This was unacceptable, so a weeding-out process had been devised. Because of the numbers and the limitations of time, when we lined up to face the *makiwara* we could only hit it a few times before making way for the student behind. Everyone was very happy, but the seniors were not! Anyway, every afternoon the karate class went for a three kilometre run to Gokoku-ji [Gokoku temple], and the last two back were asked to stop their karate training. These runs were hard, even though I had strong legs gained from rugby, because no one wanted the ignominy of being asked to leave, so the pace of the race was brisk to say the least. After the race we trained. It wasn't long before the class had been whittled down to about thirty, and when we moved to the new *dojo*, about forty, and this meant we could practise properly. Then we could hit the *makiwara* many more times!

"The normal karate class was in the afternoon, and all the members of the Takushoku club trained then; it was only the inside students that trained first thing in the morning and in the evening. We trained twice as much as the normal student. Therefore the selected students, the dormitory students, tended to be very good *karateka*.

"The morning session was always *kihon*, many, many times, *oi-zuki, gyaku-zuki, age-uke, ude-uke, uchi-uke*, and so on. Also, *ippon-kumite* and a great deal of *gohon-kumite*. *Gohon-kumite* is very simple, but also very hard. It was rarely a case of 1 .. 2 .. 3 .. 4 .. 5, in an ordered fashion with equal timing between moves; no, the seniors would attack, perhaps, 1 .. 2 .. 3,4,5, or 1 .. 2,3 .. 4,5. They could do any combination, and you never knew when they were going to punch. Another thing they did was, instead of blocking and countering on the last move, they'd dispense with the block and deliver a *chudan mae-geri*, and they weren't averse to making contact either. We had to put up with it because they were our seniors. It wasn't training, as we know it today, it was bullying, plain and simple.

"The afternoon sessions were not unlike the karate we do today. We would start with *kihon* and then progress to *kumite* and finish with *kata*. These lessons were mostly agreeable and nothing like as hard as the inside students had to endure.

"In the evenings, the Old Boys, past graduates, would come and train, and these sessions could be very demanding. Each Old Boy had his own ideas, and the lessons were very unpredictable. As I've mentioned before, this happened two nights a week. In the winter it was bitterly cold, you couldn't feel your feet. One day a senior came up to me and asked whether I was cold. 'Yes, I am cold,' I replied. 'Okay,' he said, in a soft and very friendly voice, 'I'll make you warm.' He went away and came back with a long stick. He made me jump and tuck my legs up from the squat position as he swung the stick round. If the stick hit me, it really hurt, so I was under great physical and mental pressure, and it wasn't long before the sweat was dripping off me. After what seemed like an eternity, the senior said in that deceptive voice of his, grinning all the time, 'You are warm now?' I learned, and the next time he asked me whether I was cold, I answered, 'No.' But he touched my forehead and said, 'But there is no sweat!' It was a no-win situation, and out came the stick again. It was bullying all right, but you couldn't let them win.

"Today, the Japanese are taller than fifty years ago, but when I was at university I was considered tall at five foot eight and a half inches [1.74 m]. One senior would get us to line up and would shout, 'Keep lower! Hips down!' and proceeded to walk along the line of students with a stick held out just above the heads of those students who were of average height trying their utmost to sink. I was taller and my head stuck up above the rest, even though I was, relative to my size, as low in the hips as my colleagues. This fact didn't seem to be appreciated though, and that stick would just come along and ... bang!

"I recall one Old Boy, Uchida *San*, who would get us to run along a wall in the *dojo*, literally run on the side of the wall. We had to defy gravity, ninja style. He was a small person, and his karate was not notable, though he was 2nd Dan I think, but he had some interesting ideas. At first, I could only perform one or two steps along the wall, and then came down, but after more practise, much more practise, I could do seven or eight steps before gravity got the better of me. I found this type of training refreshing, and it made me think. We enjoyed this practice not only because it was novel, but also because it made a very pleasant change from the usual hard slog. We would practise ourselves every day. I think that even in the hardest *dojo* it is good to have a break occasionally, otherwise narrow-mindedness can easily set in.

"Mister Hidetaka Nishiyama, a former Takushoku karate captain, would come along on these evening sessions regularly. His training was always very hard. [In 1952, Nishiyama was twenty-fours years of age, with nine years of karate training behind him]. The students would all be in the *dojo*, waiting, and we would know in advance who was going to teach that evening by the sound of the instructor's footsteps as he approached the *dojo*. When Nishiyama's footsteps were heard our hearts used to sink a little, for we all knew that we were going to sweat. Nishiyama was not forgiving to students. I found him to have a sharp mind, but to be dry and aloof. His style was very strong and crisp. He performed a good *Tekki Sandan*. In 1953 he went as part of a team [seven *judoka* and three *karateka*], sponsored by the American Airforce to tour the SAC air bases in the USA and Cuba for four months, so during this time we had a little rest from Mr. Nishiyama!

"I also remember Mr. Arai, Mr. Minoda and Mr. Yasuo Yanase. Mister Minoda was taller than me and very strong; we were all frightened of him. Mister Yanase was also a 4th Dan in judo. He was also a powerful man. They were all working for companies; they weren't professional *karateka*. I think Nishiyama, Arai and Yanase were 3rd Dans in karate at the time. When he left at the end of my first year, Mr. Okazaki would come and teach us as well. After the first year, Masatoshi Nakayama *Sensei* would also come along. He was a 5th Dan, and he looked stern and hard. He rarely joked and was very serious. However, looks can be misleading, and he was a very kind and intelligent person, and we used to like his lessons. He would explain technical points in great detail, in a scientific way, and we were able to enjoy this. His lessons were always

Master Hidetaka Nishiyama

disciplined, very correct, but not as physically demanding as other seniors. "The real reason why we enjoyed Nakayama *Sensei's* lessons was because the 'Why' of karate was explained to us. With other seniors, I would sometimes ask a question, and they'd hit me! That was the old

Master Masatoshi Nakayama

way, we were expected just to follow blindly, to do what we were told, and discover for ourselves. This system had good points as well as bad points. For example, we naturally acquired great speed, fighting speed, to defend ourselves and for *tai-sabaki*, but the essential bad point was that we were unable to build upon what others had learned. If a particular movement could be performed a better way, it might take ten years for a student to discover, and that could have been noted on day one. On the other hand, too much explaining is not good either, too much talk produces lazy students, and so a middle way is best. With hindsight, it was the constant practise of basic techniques that made our technique what it was. Boredom comes to all students of karate, it certainly came to me many times as a student, but if you are able to continue training, beat yourself, then the benefits of karate will open up before you. A *karateka* must see it through.

"Minoru Miyata would very occasionally come and teach us. He was based on Kyushu. He was two years junior to Nakayama at Takushoku, but they held the same grade. Miyata was really strong. His favourite stance was *fudo-dachi*, which he learned from Yoshitaka [Gichin Funakoshi's third son] at the Shotokan *dojo*. All the students noticed that Miyata and Nakayama had different form, but we never

Master Minoru Miyata

said anything. It was only later that I learned that their backgrounds were different, but it was at this time that I began to formulate in my mind that 'Shotokan 'pure' does not exist.'[7]

"When Yoshitaka first came to Japan, I was told that his karate was not notable, so his father sent him back to Okinawa to study, as Gichin Funakoshi was getting on, in his mid sixties, and he wanted to ensure the next generation. When Yoshitaka came back to Tokyo however, his style was very different from his father's. Yoshitaka used *fudo-dachi* instead of *zenkutsu-dachi*; he never used *zenkutsu-dachi*. Yoshitaka believed that *fudo-dachi* was a more natural stance, a more relaxed stance. He believed that the straight back leg of *zenkutsu-dachi* was not natural, as the stance was designed solely for the instant. Yoshitaka trained very hard, and at the time, at Takushoku, we believed that such exertion killed him. [Yoshitaka had been diagnosed with tuberculosis from the age of seven, and actually died of gangrene of the lungs on the 24th November, 1945, aged thirty-nine]. We heard many, many stories about Yoshitaka, but we never really knew whether they were true or not.

"Mister Nishiyama was known for his punching ability. Yanase was an expert at throwing because of his judo, so you learned not to get too close. He was very difficult to partner; he was a special person. Minoda and Arai were kicking specialists. I remember Arai's *mawashi-geri*, that was something to behold, and Minoda would perform a *jodan mawashi-geri* but deliberately miss the presumed target, and hook his instep behind his opponent's head and hold him like that while he punched. That required tremendous centering and balance. They were all wonderful *karateka*, and Takushoku had an envious and fearsome reputation amongst the university karate clubs.

"When I look back, some funny things happened in that first year at Takushoku too. I had never been with a woman before, had sex, and my seniors took me to a *joroya* [prostitute], not a geisha, so that I might be initiated. They ordered me to; I had no option. I was very nervous; my legs were shaking. I went into the room, and my seniors waited outside. Dear me, it was very difficult, but I had to make a go of it otherwise I'd have never heard the end of it. Just when I had taken my clothes off and was about to start, my seniors knocked on the door. I could detect an air of joviality in their voices. 'Kanazawa! Have you finished yet? Let's go!' they called. '*Oss*! ... No!' I replied, rather worriedly, 'I haven't started yet.' This untimely interruption spoilt the condition of my manly attribute – my penis drooped. I finally got going again, and just as I was about to conclude the purpose of my visit, there came another, more impatient knock on the door. 'Kanazawa! Have you finished *now*?' Oh! My seniors' timing was very poor!" The author then asked the master whether his seniors ever took him back to see this or other *joroya*. His reply was wonderful: "No! When we [the other first-year students] knew where to go, we went there on our own!"

Master Kanazawa continued: "Things were rather different in those days. Because of the very hard karate training and the studies, one never had time to build a relationship with a woman. It just wasn't possible. Many *karateka*, perhaps most, I don't know, used *joroya* to vent a natural need.

"The seniors could certainly be cruel! I remember another time when Terada and I – we were always together – went to visit Mr. Kurosawa, an Old Boy, whose family business was forestry, the trees being cut for railway sleepers and for charcoal. Kurosawa was very strong. When he saw us, he was genuinely pleased. 'Welcome! Welcome!' he said. He asked us about training, and insisted that we should train now we were there. Terada and I looked at each other, for there was no *dojo* to be seen. We changed into our *gi* at his request and were taken to an enormous field that seemed to stretch as far as the eye could see, and that was full of cows. '*Oi-zuki*!' Kurosawa said, and instructed us to perform lunge-punches across the field. It wasn't long before we were doing our best to avoid, not always successfully I might add, the cowpats. After a while, I came across a cow that wouldn't move, so I *oi-zuki*'d around her. Kurosawa was watching us all the time, but later we thought he couldn't possibly see us as we'd *oi-zuki*'d so far and we couldn't see him, so we walked to the far end of the field and walked back to where we thought he might be able to see us again, and then performed proper *oi-zuki*. The trip took us an hour.

"When we got back, Kurosawa demanded, 'One more time!' I implored him, but he wouldn't have it, and off we went again. As we *oi-zuki*'d our way across the field, we thought that he must have been able to see us walking, so we resolved to do the labour honestly this time. We went in a straight line, paying no heed to the cowpats, or the large mosquitoes that seemed to swarm in that field. We got bitten many, many times, but we couldn't avoid it, because we were performing the punches with good form. We went across the whole field lunge-punching and then turned and came back. On the way back, a cow was once again in my way and refused to budge as I came towards it. 'Perhaps,' I thought, 'Kurosawa objected to me giving way to the cow last time, and didn't see us walking at all?' So I was resolved to go straight. When I got to the cow, it looked straight at me, as much as to say that it wasn't going to move. Although a bit wary, because cows can be frisky at times, and, as I've explained, I had no great affinity with farm animals, I touched it, lightly, with my fist. 'Please excuse me,' I implored, and with a long and laborious 'Moooo...,' she wandered off.

"Kurosawa had been watching us all the time through binoculars. He asked us to perform this labour because he wanted to instill in us that, whilst daunting, crossing that enormous field was possible.

"I recall another visit that Terada and I made to another Takushoku Old Boy, Ryohei Myojyo, who lived on the island of Shikoku. I nearly didn't survive this trip, however. We arrived at Myojyo's, and shortly afterwards I had a very bad pain in my abdomen. Myojyo said that I should train, which was the last thing I felt like doing, but, as usual, I obeyed my senior. But the pain grew worse, and Myojyo then suggested I should eat rice cake, which I did. By now I was in severe pain, and Myojyo thought that I should drink, but the pain just got worse still. More food and more drink followed, but eventually I had to go to the hospital. It turned out that I had acute appendicitis, and there was no time to delay. It was such a hurry in fact, that the nurse forgot to shave me, and I did not, of course, have the customary period of fasting and lack of drinking before an operation. The doctor said that I nearly died, and that I had to stay in hospital for seven days, but I had karate commitments and I discharged myself after four. I told the hospital administrators that I was from Okinawa, as a joke, I can't remember why now, but when payment for my care came from home, they noticed it was from Honshu. They were really cross with me because it meant more admin' for them. Myojyo is dead now.

"I also remember Takushoku Old Boys Susumu Nishimura, who is still living in Okayama Prefecture, and Keiji Kikuchi, from Sendai, who was president of a transport company and a former president of Takushoku Old Boys; also, a very great senior, Shinji Moritaka from Kyushu, who is still alive. I also remember Takashi Naka, from Hosei, who is dead now too.

"I recall when the karate club went on a trip by train, perhaps to a summer camp. In the carriage corridor, we passed the conductor in single file, with the most senior students at the front and the most junior at the rear. The conductor wanted our fares, and as we passed him, each student would turn to his classmate walking behind and say to the conductor, 'He'll pay.' I was last in the line, and when I got to the conductor I said the leader would pay. The conductor, who was a friend of a senior, would have nothing of it. 'You are a First Year junior!' he exclaimed, 'You must not cheat!' So, I bowed, and got caught for paying all the fares. You learned quickly at Takushoku!

"After six months I was a 6th kyu. 9th kyu and 8th kyu could be awarded, the system allowed for this, but you couldn't take an

Master Ryohei Myojyo

examination for these. If a student trained hard, then they were usually awarded 7th kyu or 6th kyu. We trained every single day and graded every six months. The grading was much as it is today, though we didn't

Master Susumu Nishimura   Master Keiji Kikuchi

change belt colour, and at 6th kyu we still wore white. At the next grading, after one year of training, I was graded to 3rd kyu, brown-belt. Kyu grades only wore white or brown. For university undergraduates this was okay, but in general *dojo* people like to have conspicuous recognition of grading success in the form of different colour belts, and this is particularly true of the West. If a more elaborate belt system doesn't operate, then students won't train. They need recognition of success to gain success.

"After another six months, I graded to *Shodan*. [This was an astonishingly short time. Master Kanazawa had started late at the karate class and had graded to black-belt before any others in his year. When you bear in mind the nature of the training and the standard set, this is a remarkable achievement. If a student trained hard, two years of practice was normally required in a university noted for its fanatical dedication].

"My *Shodan* grading was hard, of course. I took it towards the end of 1953 at the Takushoku *dojo*. It was a JKA *Dan* grading for a number of universities – Waseda, Chuo, Hosei, Keio, Takushoku, and so on, who came together for the event. My examiners were Funakoshi *Sensei*; Isao Obata *Sensei*, from Keio, an original student of Funakoshi *Sensei's*, and the first chairman of the JKA; Toshio Kamata [later, Watabe (sometimes written as 'Watanabe')] *Sensei* and Hiroshi Noguchi, both

Master Shinji Moritaka

from Waseda University [see [8 & 9] for information on these two famous *karateka*], and Masatoshi Nakayama *Sensei*. Obata and Kamata were the other two *karateka* who accompanied Nishiyama to America in 1953. Kamata had been a major in the war. Noguchi *Sensei*, who had also been an officer, is eighty-eight years of age today, and was a founder member of the Waseda karate club in the early 1930s. He is still training. He was an honoured guest at the celebrations to mark twenty years of SKI. We get on very well. It was Noguchi *Sensei* who devised *gohon-kumite*. He created it from kendo.

"The point that sticks out in my mind about my *Shodan* grading was the timing of the Waseda students, which was different from that of the Takushoku students. I recall the *jiyu-ippon kumite* I had to perform. My Waseda partner landed, paused a fraction of a second, and then punched. When I attacked him, he expected me to land and punch in the same manner, but I punched as I landed, which is the Takushoku way, and I hit him hard in the face. I broke his teeth. I apologized. It was the difference in timing, that's all. Keio University had different timing still,

Master Takashi Naka

for they used to step forward and punch and then land. It was very confusing and a little dangerous!

"After all the basics, the seniors stipulated how many *jodan* and *chudan* punches we had to do, how many *mae-geri, mawashi-geri* and *kekomi* for *ippon-kumite*. It wasn't just one or two of each. The *jiyu-kumite* I enjoyed very much. It was the best part for me, I had confidence, and I felt that I could rest a little.

"My *kata* was *Bassai-Dai*. Funakoshi *Sensei* was the examiner for the *kata*. I remember that clearly. Passing a *Shodan* is just the beginning of studying karate really.

"One year later [1954] I took my *Nidan* at the Waseda *dojo*, and passed. My *kata* was *Kanku-Dai*. I don't remember that much about the grading now to be honest. But I'd like to make one point. I suppose Funakoshi watched the freestyle sparring at the gradings, because he was there. I don't think that he was opposed to it. It was competition that Funakoshi *Sensei* objected to.

"Another point that might be of interest was that Funakoshi *Sensei* always dated the Dan certificates according to the year since the Meiji restoration [1868].

"Once a month, the university karate clubs would have a training session together. I remember seeing Obata *Sensei* performing the *kata Kanku-Dai*. I thought that this was very good, very strong. He would partner Funakoshi *Sensei* in demonstrations.

"Sometimes I would go and collect Funakoshi *Sensei* from his eldest son's house, a small wooden building near the university, only about one kilometre from Takushoku. He was very old, in his mid eighties, and he had trouble walking, so I collected him by taxi. I would see a woman there, who I took to be Yoshihide's wife [Yoshihide was Funakoshi's eldest son. He had studied karate in his youth under Masters Azato and Itosu on Okinawa. He worked for a dry-cleaning company in Tokyo and died on 2nd March, 1961, aged seventy-one]. So, I would collect the master and take him to the Takushoku *dojo*. I remember on one memorable occasion, I thought to myself whilst sitting alongside him, 'He looks very old. I don't think he could block me. I don't think he could block an *uraken*.' Just at that point, immediately after my thinking this, Funakoshi *Sensei* turned to me, smiled, and said, 'Try if you want to Mr. Kanazawa! Try if you want to!' Oh! I was very surprised. Somehow he knew. Somehow he had picked up my thoughts. My belief then was the same as it is now, nearly fifty years on, that the old master was telepathic.

"On these short journeys he would talk about Jigaro Kano *Sensei* [the founder of judo]. Funakoshi respected Kano greatly. When Funakoshi came to Tokyo, Kano helped him a lot. Kano ordered his top

Master Gichin Funakoshi

students to train in karate, and also practised himself.

"I also knew Shinken Gima *Sensei*. In Japanese, his first name was Makoto. He was Funakoshi's first black-belt in Tokyo [in 1923]. Gima [who was born in 1897] was Okinawan, and had come to Tokyo to attend Hitotsubashi University. He was a clever man. I respected him very much indeed. When he came to Japan, Gima knew karate, he'd been practising ten years under Yasutsune Itosu *Sensei* and Kentsuo Yabu *Sensei*, and he partnered Funakoshi *Sensei* when he was trying to get karate established.

"Funakoshi *Sensei* was a small person with a round face and a red complexion, like an apple. It was the kind of complexion you might have if you were a drinker, but Funakoshi *Sensei* only rarely had a drink, and I understand that his colour was an Okinawan characteristic. He was of a very kind disposition, very soft, both a gentle man and a gentleman. He always wore high, heavy *geta*, and I was always fearful that he would fall over. I asked my seniors about this and they said that Funakoshi wore them to strengthen his legs. Funakoshi *Sensei* always thought about training; karate was his life.

"I only ever saw Funakoshi *Sensei* perform a *kata* once, and that was *Kanku-Dai*, which was his favourite form. The *kata* was not obviously strong, not fast, but it was very tasteful. There was something different about it that's hard to put into words – strange, yet highly polished timing. One point I noticed was the opening move. We in the JKA had always been told to bring the arms up slowly, break suddenly, and then bring the hands to the front, just like you will see today. Funakoshi *Sensei*, however, didn't perform the movement this way. He brought his hands up, but when the hands split there was no sudden break, and instead of bending the arms, they were straight. Yes, I remember that distinctly. Another point was near the end of the *kata* before the jump. After the last movement in the *Tekki*-like sequence, after the *gedan-barai* in *kiba-dachi*, we brought the left leg up and, upon landing in *kiba-dachi*, performed *ryo-ude-mawashi-uke* before the *otoshi-zuki*, but Funakoshi never brought his leg up, he simply stepped through.

"I also recall that Funakoshi *Sensei* would never *kiai* with a 'Ya!' or an 'Ah,' as we had been taught. No, he preferred to make a sound like 'Whoo.' [This is interesting, and in contrast to Egami's[10] recollection of Funakoshi's *kiai*, which he reported as being a *hoi* sound].

"As students, we wondered why we were taught one way and Funakoshi *Sensei* performed techniques and moves in other ways. Funakoshi would usually direct comments to the entire class in the *dojo*, but I recall very clearly that on one occasion he addressed me directly, and I'll never forget it. 'Mr. Kanazawa,' he said very softly, 'Please get lower and keep your stances a little wider. Keep deeper and wider.' I replied that I was trying my best to copy him. He smiled and said: 'You are a young man. I am eighty-five years old. I am an old man. I can no longer train as I would wish. You must do as I say, not as I do. I am

Master Funakoshi performing the *kata Tekki Shodan*

sorry' [for not being able to demonstrate as he would have liked]. I really respected Funakoshi *Sensei* for saying that. We thought that he was a god, that everything he did was pure, but when he said he couldn't do it, I admired him even more for it. He was a very great master. Perhaps he was the only great master who said he couldn't do it. In other styles, the students copied the old masters who weren't prepared to say they couldn't do the deep stances any longer, and so the students copied their high stances. Funakoshi *Sensei* was very truthful. So, we had to train in line with Funakoshi's request, but which is the right way I cannot say.

"After one or two years at Takushoku, someone said to me that they'd met Mr. Nagayama in Omoto. I was told that Nagayama still lived in great fear of what I was going to do to him. He worried every day. Some twelve years had elapsed since the slapping incident, and he had lived all that time knowing that I would be returning to take my revenge. It was on hearing this news that I decided that that was enough, Nagayama had paid for what he'd done to me. He'd had his punishment. I also think that I was just beginning to appreciate what *budo* was about, so I put a stop to it. Two or three years later, Nagayama died.

"Nagayama practised sumo, as I have said, and that reminds me of another incident, funny this time, about a sumo wrestler at university. In the martial arts dormitory complex at Takushoku, where the karate club was based in its entirety, inside students of the judo, boxing, European fencing and sumo clubs also resided, these other arts having *dojo* about the campus. Anyway, one of the sumo wrestlers was named Kanazawa, and he was always getting into fights. He liked fighting very much and was really strong. He'd have a fight and then escape back to the university. Once the police came round to Takushoku and arrested me by mistake. I protested my innocence, but they would hear nothing of it.

"Mind you, members of the karate club were not entirely innocent! Each university had an unofficial territory, and each was always trying to extend its territory. I remember going with some other *karateka* to northwest Tokyo, to Rikkyo University, which was outside our territory, to try and enlarge our domain. We had a few fights with the Rikkyo karate students. Normally, when friends walk along a street, they walk together in a line shoulder to shoulder, but when we went to Rikkyo, we always walked in file, one after the other, so we always had reinforcements coming up from the rear.

"It was mostly bravado of course, young men seeing what they could get away with, testing themselves, though it was conducted in all seriousness. I'll give you another example of the sort of thing we got up to. I recall that a classmate of mine, who was tall and a former Nagasaki Prefecture High School boxing champion, and I, feeling that we could hold our own in a free-for-all, once walked through the streets of Atami, famous for its spring waters, wearing kimono, and on the backs of these we had written, 'Fight us if you want to.' I had been in a few fights and I felt that I could handle myself. Luckily, no one did challenge us! We had young men's false confidence.

"Talking of territories, I remember an incident that could have got very nasty. There was a small village near where I lived and the people were fishermen who worked for my brother. They netted tuna and checked the nets two times a day. One day, they went out only to find, on arriving back, that one of their houses had been wrecked by *yakuza*. My brother was worried and asked me to see if I could sort it out, but that I should not get involved in fighting. One of my father's employees, a 4th or 5th Dan *judoka* and I went along. As we walked down the village high street, the inhabitants shut all the windows and doors, and it was just like a scene from a spaghetti western. We just hung around, and when the men were out checking the nets, one *yakuza* came. I went and talked to him. He pulled a knife and showed me some fancy work. 'Why do you challenge us?' I asked. 'We have three hundred fighters, we are ready, but we don't want trouble. Many people will get hurt. Let's you and I settle it. You can use your knife and I will use my karate. If you stab me, I will not die quickly, and may well live, but if I hit you, you will die.' The man knew I was from Takushoku, the reputation of the university was widespread, and so we shook hands and there was no problem. I think the whole thing was about territory. They wanted to expand and make the village pay for 'protection', something like that.

"Sometimes, a friend and I used to go to the shadier parts of Tokyo. We wore JKA jumpers, with JKA written on them, and in the evenings we turned the jumpers inside out so we couldn't be identified. We sometimes goaded the local thugs and then claimed self-defence. It was just youthful enthusiasm, but if Nakayama had known about it, we'd have been out!

"Every year at university, we had a summer school, a *gasshuku*, which lasted one week. In my first year we went to Kujukuriga-hama, a noted beach many kilometres in length, in Chiba Prefecture, about eighty kilometres northeast of Tokyo. In those days it was a small fishing resort, but now it has become very popular with tourists. After training, we would help the fisherman drag in the nets, and as a reward they'd give us a few fish to cook. Although there were many types of fish, the most common was the blue-backed horse mackerel. We stayed in a temple, sleeping and cooking there. In the mornings we trained on the beach at six o'clock, and we used to run, which was very tiring because of the soft sand. The morning sessions were for one and a half hours. Then we'd have breakfast, and then we'd practise from half-past nine to half-past eleven. Lunch followed, and then we trained from two-thirty to five o'clock in a school gym the university had rented. At five o'clock we had dinner, and in the evenings we had lectures. The seniors would talk to us about many things, mostly karate of course. The purpose was to motivate us to do greater things. I remember one story a senior told us, I don't want to mention his name, about when Nakayama was in Manchuria. This senior told us that a soldier had told Nakayama that he had been ordered to kill someone. The soldier didn't want to use a gun or a sword for some reason, so he had carried out his orders using a karate technique.

"That reminds me of Morihana, a famous Old Boy of the university, who had died in the war. He was a legend at Takushoku. He was tall, handsome, with a perfect body, but he was noted for his fantastic kicking ability. He was also very strong, and many stories were told at Takushoku about Morihana to inspire us. I regret that I cannot remember any of them now, though I believe that he did not wish to leave a comrade and died as a consequence, from disease I think. This was seen as heroic.

"Another famous Old Boy was Mr. Isao Fukui. He was very strong as well, and especially noted for his freestyle. He is still alive, practising karate, and is an adviser to the Japan Karate Federation.

"Because the training at the *gasshuku* was so hard, the First Years looked forward to preparing meals because we avoided training the previous session! We were worn-out at the end of each day, absolutely worn-out.

"Many Old Boys came to that *gasshuku*. I remember that someone, a student senior, wanted to frighten Nakayama *Sensei*, to play a trick on him. Nakayama didn't like snakes, so this senior picked up a blue-green snake and put it into his bed. It wasn't poisonous, the only snake in Japan that is venomous is the *mamushi,* but Nakayama was frightened of snakes, poisonous or otherwise. We were humble First Years, so we just kept quiet. We had all been training in the afternoon, and Nakayama went to bed to rest when we got back. After a short while we heard, 'Yaaaaa...' Nakayama *Sensei* was a very senior *karateka*, and I said to myself, 'He's frightened of snakes?' I was very surprised.

"I remember, later, going to the baths with Nakayama *Sensei*. He was walking in front of me and he suddenly stopped, froze. 'There!' he whispered, 'over there,' pointing to ground. It was dark and I couldn't see anything. 'Over there!' he said again, with more insistence. I went to where he was pointing, and on the ground was a very small, harmless snake. '*Oss!*' I replied, and picked it up and brought it over, with a view to putting it down on some grass. 'What are you doing?' Nakayama shouted. He was very alarmed. When I explained, he said I must not bring it near him. It was really a very tiny snake.

"However, I could empathise with Nakayama, because I was frightened of dogs. When I was at school, elementary school I think, I was about eleven years old, I would take Esu out for a walk. This region is a lovely part of Japan, and where I lived is now part of the Rikuchu-Kaigan National Park. Often I would throw one of my wooden *geta* into the Omoto River, or the ocean, and he'd jump in and retrieve it. Sometimes he'd give it back to me, sometimes he'd run home, and I had to walk back with only the remaining *geta* on! Anyway, one day, on such a walk, a large truck passed by, the type with an open rear, and in the back were five construction labourers. One of the men shouted something at me, something insulting, for absolutely no reason. I let the dog off the lead, shouted, 'Esu! Attack!' and thought that he would simply chase the truck. But he didn't. He jumped up into the back and attacked that man who had shouted at me. It was a serious attack and it really frightened me. How did Esu know to attack that particular man? It is a question I have often asked myself, as is how he knew about Nagayama. He had been well trained, for he had been a police dog. One of my elder brothers had got him from the police station. After the attack, I was very frightened and ran off home. When I got back, Esu had already returned. My father had to pay compensation, and said that I shouldn't let the dog off the lead again. He didn't scold me; he just said that an animal is very honest.

"The second summer school was held in Ibaragi Prefecture. I cannot remember the exact location now, maybe Oarai beach, but we stayed in a boarding house near the city of Mito, about two hundred kilometres north of Tokyo. About the same number of students went to Mito as went to Kujukuriga-hama, around sixty, which was a lot. In my third and fourth summer camps, the numbers were far less. The training that second year was the same as for the previous year; it never differed very much. It was always hard! The captain of the karate club that year was Oishi [not Takeshi Oishi, the four times JKA individual *kumite* champion], who was studying commercial science, like me, and the vice-captain was Hiroshi Shoji. Oishi was very strict, disciplined and focused. He was a 2nd Dan like Okazaki, and it was usual for a person of this quality to graduate and then receive 3rd Dan. Shoji, who was a 1st Dan at the time, has become a famous *karateka* of course. He was two years my senior. He was more relaxed than Mr. Oishi, and a very quiet, modest, and serious man.

"It was difficult that second year for the seniors to control the juniors, because there were too many First Years and they all had confidence. Looking back, the juniors were lacking in discipline. Our seniors started karate at university, but many, many of the new intake had studied karate at High School and had actually trained longer than the seniors. Some came to Takushoku as black-belts, but like other universities, they had to start again, as white-belts.

"There was trouble that year because of the fighting between the First Years and local troublemakers, *yakuza*, in Mito one night. After lectures, the students were given an hour off, and Mito was the only attraction. The trouble wasn't caused by drink. Oishi said that no one should drink. I think a few did secretly, but it was only the odd nip. I don't know how the fight started, but the police couldn't stop it. The Takushoku seniors had to go down and we had a word with the juniors. They trusted us and we said that we wouldn't mention the incident to the captain and vice-captain if they left, and so they did.

"Nearly every year there would be two or three students who would run away from the summer camp, because they couldn't endure the rigour, the harshness of the training. Of course, they couldn't escape, for we had their addresses, everything. When we got back to Tokyo, we would meet up with these individuals again, because whereas they might be able to run from the summer camp, they could not run from their academic studies if they wanted their degree. We would give these escapees a party, a certain kind of party, to mark their retirement from the karate club. These parties were called *taibu-matsuri*. Firstly, the 'guests' were obliged to bunny-hop around the *dojo* a minimum of five times and often seven times, which was extremely gruelling. Sometimes, they would collapse, and a senior would throw a bucket of cold water over them to get them going again.

"After the bunny-hops had been completed, and they were always completed, the 'guests' had to do freestyle with four or five seniors. Sometimes, the seniors would put towels around their fists and hit those that had gone absent without leave. Often, the juniors would be knocked out or badly injured, then the bucket of cold water would be thrown over them again, and they'd have to carry on fighting. Some of these people nearly died. When the freestyle was over they were asked to leave the karate club in no uncertain terms.

"Often, the 'guests' declined the invitation to their farewell party, but we always went to collect them; they always attended *taibu-matsuri*, the celebration, whether they wanted to or not.

"Personally, I didn't want to get too involved in this type of thing, it

Master Masataka Mori and Master Kanazawa at Takushoku University – 1953

wasn't necessarily my idea of what to do, and if proceedings were getting out of hand I told my classmates they'd better stop.

"This type of thing doesn't happen today. I think it's because the young people aren't strong enough; they lack endurance and spirit. In our time, people were stronger. [This is no doubt true, but the fanaticism of some of the students at Takushoku led to consequences that some might argue went far beyond the acceptable. Clive Nicol, who started training at the JKA in 1962, reported a case in his *Moving Zen* (Paul Crompton, 1975) of a student who wished to discontinue karate training and, being ordered to attend the club by a senior for one last practice, was beaten so badly that he died].

"The third year summer school was held in Fukui City, I can't remember exactly where it was held now, but we stayed in a temple again, in the suburbs. It was a train journey of about four hundred kilometres southwest of Tokyo. I was a *Nidan* by now and had respect. The captain was Mr. Masataka Mori, who is now based in New York. I think he studied political economy, but I'm not sure. The vice-captain was Nakamura, who now runs a monthly magazine, *Gekkan Karate-Do*. The Third Year students, of whom I was one, tended to teach and manage the juniors. I think that was the year that Mr. Keinosuke Enoeda, who came from Fukuoka, Kyushu, and classmate, Mr. Tetsuhiko Asai, from Shikoku, started at Takushoku.

"The point that I remember most about my third *gasshuku* was the exchange training with another university. I'm almost certain it was Ritsumeikan, from Kyoto, where they practised Goju-ryu under Gogen Yamaguchi, the famous Cat, who had been a student at the university twenty-five years before. [Yamaguchi was born in Kagoshima, Kyushu, in 1909]. I knew Yamaguchi *Sensei* because I had trained under him as a student at his *dojo* in Asakusa, near Ueno, in Tokyo, a very popular location, noted for its Endo style buildings. The policy at Takushoku was that you were encouraged to visit other *dojo* and to keep the good points you had learned.

"I was impressed with Yamaguchi *Sensei*. He looked very fierce, like a samurai with his shoulder-length hair, and he was very strong, very good. When we watched him training, we would never dare talk – we were frightened. However, if you went up to him outside the *dojo* and said '*Oss*!' and spoke to him, he always had a big smile on his face and was polite – a really nice person. I remember Yamaguchi performing many *kata*, especially *Tensho* and *Sanchin*. He was powerful, and he used to remove his *gi* top to show how to breathe properly and demonstrate correct muscular tension.

"One of my classmates was Kokichi Matsushima. He had studied Itosu-ryu under Kinjo *Sensei* and was always strong. I used to accompany him to other *dojo* for exchange training. I visited Yamaguchi's *dojo* during my first two years at Takushoku.

"Takushoku and Ritsumeikan were great rivals. I remember sparring with one of their members and one of my seniors shouted after a clash, where I had kicked my opponent, 'You must control Kanazawa!' so that all could hear. I carried on fighting showing greater control. Then, during an interval, the senior who had issued the warning came up and quietly whispered to me, 'Why are you controlling?' He wanted the assembled *karateka* to think one thing and encouraged me to do the exact opposite. These exchange matches were bloody affairs; very little control seemed to be exercised or encouraged. I found this to be particularly true when the exchanges were between two different styles – Shotokan and Shito-ryu, Shotokan and Wado-ryu, and so on. When the exchange matches were held between two Shotokan universities, the competition was fierce, but there weren't so many injuries – the honour of the university was at stake, but not the style as well!

"Afterwards, a Goju-ryu senior from Ritsumeikan came up to me and asked if he could see my kicks. I showed him and we paired-up. I attacked him and he stepped back. He did this a number of times, eight or nine times I suppose, and then Bang! He got my timing, and then sidestepped and caught me with *furi-uchi*, a pendulum strike, using the back of the hand.

"When Yamaguchi *Sensei* died [20th May, 1989] his third son, Goshi, went to Tokyo from New York to look after the *dojo*; the eldest son, Gosei, stayed in San Francisco teaching karate. He became a student at Takushoku studying commerce and Russian, but left after two years. The training at Takushoku was very hard, but he was expected to train under his father as well! I think he became ill. The second son lived in Germany and worked for Japan Airlines. He also taught karate, but he is dead now.

"I remember an incident with Gosei. I partnered him, but he wasn't sure about Shotokan practice, and, during *ippon-kumite* he blocked *age-uke* and then punched me in the face. I think he expected me to block. One of my upper teeth, an incisor, was knocked out, and I picked it up off the floor, slipped it back in my gum, and held it in place. The whole tooth didn't come out, for it separated, cracked inside the gum. I kept it in place all day, and for the weeks that followed, and had to be very careful how I ate, but it went black and died. Then, after six months, it began to whiten – there was life again! This happened when I was in my second year at Takushoku. It is secure now, though it still moves and is not as white as its neighbours. An x-ray still shows the break.

"I went to many other *dojo* as well, not just Yamaguchi *Sensei's*. I also visited Hironori Ohtsuka, the founder of Wado-ryu. I found Wado-ryu quite interesting for historical reasons, because Ohtsuka had been a student of Funakoshi *Sensei's* during the 1920s and early 1930s. [Ohtsuka was born in 1892, the son of a doctor. A former bank employee, he combined Shindo Yoshin Ryu Jujutsu with Shotokan to form Wado-ryu]. In some ways Wado-ryu looked similar to Shotokan, but in other ways it looked different. I thought that Shito-ryu looked more like the karate the JKA were practising. I saw Kenwa Mabuni just before he died. I thought he was like a god. His *kata* was beautiful, truly beautiful. [Mabuni was born in 1889 and learned Shuri-te from Itosu and Naha-te from Kanryo Higaonna. A police officer, he settled in Osaka shortly after Funakoshi's arrival in Tokyo. Mabuni combined Shuri-te and Naha-te to form Shito-ryu, which influenced the development of Shotokan. He died on the 23rd May, 1952, aged sixty-three].

"I saw Masutatsu Oyama the founder of Kyokushinkai, and a former student at Takushoku, training at Yamaguchi's *dojo*. I remember when Oyama bent a coin between two fingers during a demonstration. Many people said that it was a trick, but I was impressed. Later, in Hawaii, I saw him take the top off a bottle with *shuto*, and cut himself as he went through the bottle's neck. I've never had the desire to try that. The writer, Ikki Kajiwara made Oyama famous. Oyama's external appearance was like a star, a showman, but when you spoke to him he was quiet and very polite. [Oyama (real name Choi Young-Li), was born in Korea in on the 27th July, 1923. He entered Takushoku in 1941 studying Shotokan and came under the influence of Master Sodeiju. Oyama died on the 26th April, 1994, aged seventy].

"I saw many famous *Sensei* at this time. One that comes to mind was Shigeru Egami, who later became chief instructor to the Shotokai. He looked very special. An aura surrounded him, a presence. He was intense. I thought he looked like a mystic. He was very strong spiritually, close to God. He was a disciple of Funakoshi [from 1933] and was featured in the photographs to the second edition of Funakoshi's *Karate-Do Kyohan* [in 1958]. Nakayama was physical and spiritual, but Egami was more spiritual, and you can see this from his writings. [Egami died on the 8th January, 1981, aged sixty-eight. For factual information and a number of stories about Egami, see [8, 9 & 10]].

"We also trained in a number of weapons, *sai, bo,* and so on. We were mainly taught these by the seniors and Old Boys. It was just to show us the possibilities of the weapons really. Also, in the past, karate was part of Okinawan *kobudo*, but through Funakoshi, karate gained its independence, as it were. The intention of training with these weapons was to get into the mind of the warrior ancestors and to feel what they had felt. This is important for the spirit and for understanding, but we didn't become too involved with these weapons, because life is short and we had chosen Karate-Do as our means of gaining deeper insight. Budo and *bujitsu* are different. We noticed how similar the basic movements of these weapons were to the basic methods of karate movement. We found that we could pick up their techniques without too much difficulty. I found this very interesting, and it added to my belief of a common chord running through the traditional arts. 'All students of Karate-do should also learn from *kobudo* ... In many Karate-do *kata* we will find a lot of self-defence techniques against a *bo* ... The relationship of Karate-do and *kobudo* is like the wheels on a car – one cannot function without the other.'[11]

"I was the vice-captain of the karate club in my fourth year along with a student called Yoshiki Habu, like the venomous snake on Okinawa; the names are pronounced the same, but the characters are different. Habu is now a Professor of Japanese in a Malaysian University. Mister Kiyoshi Fujimoto was club captain.

A brief respite during a karate demonstration tour on Kyushu – 1955

"It was about this time, in my third or fourth year at Takushoku, that Yasuo died. I was away at the time travelling with a karate group on the northern island of Hokkaido. I received notice, a telegram from my family, that Yasuo, who had supported my change to Takushoku, as I've said, was very close to death, and that I should go back home. I decided that I could not go because I would let the group down, so I wrote a telegram. My eldest brother was very angry.

"The group was staying in a hotel, and there were five of us sleeping in one room. The night Yasuo died, I woke up and saw a figure dressed in a white kimono standing by my bed. At first, I thought this was my friend, Hiroshi Okura, because he wore a white kimono and I called out, 'Okura! What are you doing? What are you doing?' But there was no answer. The figure was still standing there, looking at me. 'Okura! What are you doing?' I called again, more forcefully. Then Okura sat up in bed and answered, 'Why are you calling me?' I replied, 'If you are over there, who is over here?' Then the white figure just seemed to fade away in front of my eyes.

"The following day, at the next hotel, I was asleep and I felt something heavy on my chest, a great pressure. At first I thought that one of the group was trying to get something from their luggage that was stored above me, and that his foot was on me. The pressure was considerable and my muscles were tight. I yelled out, 'There is someone on my bed!' The other members of the group immediately woke up and saw a figure pressing down on me. I think that this is important; there were witnesses. The figure, as if caught by a draught, was pulled out of the window and vanished. It just seemed to glide out of the open window. We thought at first that it might have been a thief, but our room was far too high up to jump out of, much too high, it was impossible, and there was no means of climbing. No, I am convinced that the two figures were one and the same, my brother, Yasuo. I saw Yasuo's ghost, and so had others. I wasn't frightened, because I had nothing to fear from my brother. I had never believed in ghosts, but those incidents convinced me otherwise. I had hoped his ghost might reappear a third time, but it never did. Yasuo and I were closely bound. He looked after me as a child. Because I couldn't go to him on his deathbed, I think he came to me to say goodbye. Even now, nearly half a century on, in a lonely hotel room somewhere in the world, I sometimes think of Yasuo.

"I believe that when I die I will meet my brother again. I feel this deep within. He was the only one who appeared to me, Shin and Chuichi never visited me, but I shall meet them also. Life is a circle. When you die, your remains are placed in, or on the earth. If you are buried, then your remains are lowered into the earth; if you are cremated, then your ashes are either scattered on the earth, or placed in it. An apple tree, for example, might take up the goodness of your remains, and people pick and eat the apples – energy circulates. In Japan, in the past, when a body was cremated, the remains made contact with the ground, but today in Japan, it is common practice for the ashes to be placed in an urn. This is no good, for the body does not go back to nature in the way intended. You must keep one small bone here [pointing to the neck], which looks like Buddha in *zazen* for our human memory, and return the ashes to the land or ocean. When I die, I don't mind if I'm buried or cremated, as long as my physical remains touch the earth again. I would like my ashes scattered over farmland so that they might nourish the crops, or taken out and scattered into the Pacific. The spirit is not affected by earth, fire or water, the body and the spirit are completely different, so no worries.

"The fourth *gasshuku* was held in Matsushima, Miyagi Prefecture. There was trouble with the First Years again, taunting and fighting the local hooligans. Nakayama *Sensei* would come to every summer school. Sometimes he would stay the week, sometimes three or four days. Nakayama's technique was very sharp and he performed a good *Tekki*

Sandan, the old way. However, even when he was in his early forties, he couldn't kick *jodan*. At the time, I thought it was because he was much older, but I found that forty years of age was no barrier to flexibility. I found I could keep very supple until sixty, though after that I began to notice that maintaining such flexibility was more of a job. I don't know why Nakayama didn't kick *jodan*, perhaps he was just stiff, and then again, perhaps he didn't want to?

"The students always liked Nakayama's *gasshuku* training, and when he went back there was always a groan of discontent. I remember that when I was in my second year, in late [December] 1954, Nakayama and Okazaki went to Thailand to teach Shotokan for two weeks, but stayed two months. The Governor of Thailand had invited the JKA to instruct the Thai army, police and university students. It was the first time the JKA had officially taught abroad, and that was important. I think the Thai reaction gave encouragement to all those who wanted karate to spread outside Japan. But for us students at the time, the two months were just one long groan, for with most of the other seniors, it was just a case of repetition – techniques again, and again, and again, hundreds of times, and nothing was ever really explained. The sole aim of the seniors was to make the karate harder, more powerful, through physical exertion. That's all I wanted to do at that stage as well. Young men you see, we didn't understand karate at all.

"In my fourth year, I shaved my head like the beginners, which surprised everybody. As I've said before, I'd escaped the First Year cut because of my late beginning. I don't remember now why I had my hair cut, but I do recall being thought of as a new member a few times because of it!

"The winter training camps were hard too, and I attended four of these. Although we were based at the university, we used to run with bare feet on the snow and ice covered roads, sometimes two kilometres, sometimes four kilometres, depending on how the senior felt each morning. Our feet would go red, then blue. Yes, I remember that!

"I broke many bones at university – fingers, both hands, both arms, my right shoulder, feet and toes – but in my fourth year I had a very narrow escape with my neck. I was instructing and the students were very tired so I gave them a rest, during which time we exercised a little with a partner. One student would sit on the floor, and the other would gently twist their partner's neck, with one hand on the jaw gently moving in one direction, and the other hand on the head pulling in the other direction. My partner, Misumi, was a First Year, and, despite my instruction to do the manoeuvre gently, in a relaxed manner, he jerked my head far

During a visit to Miyako, when Master Kanazawa led a karate *gasshuku* and a series of demonstrations – 1955.

too hard. My head went further than it should have, and it stayed there, locked. I couldn't move it back for six months. I went to the hospital and the doctor who attended me said that I was lucky to be alive. There was nothing they could do; it just had to heal naturally, with time. I had to sleep in one position only. Training was very difficult of course, as I was punching in one direction and my head was facing nearly ninety degrees in another direction. I could only really see what I was doing with one eye.

"Blocking kicks usually caused most injuries. That's how the majority of my breaks occurred. I also had quite a few stitches over my right eye and right ear. But, of course, some injuries were self-inflicted! The worst self-inflicted injury I received was to my back. I performed a *jodan mawashi-geri* and then I jumped up, spun round in mid air, and kicked with the other leg, *yoko-geri-keage*. It was a bad idea and a bad kick. It must have looked like it had come out of a movie! I was experimenting and I got the timing wrong. After I landed, I couldn't move. I literally couldn't move. Even breathing was very painful. I passed out. Someone revived me and the doctor came and he gave me a pain-killing injection in the back. This happened in the countryside, and I don't think the doctor really knew what to do. I managed somehow to get back to

Tokyo on the train, yet despite the painkiller the journey was excruciatingly painful; I felt every jolt. I couldn't stand up and I couldn't sit down, so I lay on the luggage rack above the seats, which acted rather like a hammock that swung with every movement. I managed a little relief from my pain. The other passengers were very surprised!

"When I reached Tokyo I went straight to the hospital and they said that one of the vertebrae had become displaced, and that it was not the jumping kick that had done it as such, but rather it had happened many years before and the kick had weakened the vertebra's position sufficiently for it to go out of place. For two or three days I couldn't move, and I was severely restricted for two weeks and by the third week I was beginning to move more freely. When I started training again, I was generally okay, but occasionally – Ah! I found that I needed to spend a long time loosening up before training, and considerable time warming down after training, which is a good idea in any case.

"When I was younger, because of all these injuries, I was in constant discomfort, sometimes pain, but when I reached sixty years of age, all the pain and discomfort ceased. I have no arthritis or anything like that. It is very strange, but very welcome. I also lost my fear of dogs. I believe that, if it wasn't for the constant travelling around the world, I could quite easily live to one hundred and twenty-five, but the travelling, passing so many time zones so frequently, is very disruptive to the body's rhythms. If I continue as I am now, I have great confidence that I shall live to be one hundred years old, and karate will have given me that.

"I remember when Mr. Gima wrote a foreword for one of my books. He was very kind and said that the two young *karateka* that impressed him were [Tsutomo] Ohshima and myself. But I was fifty years old at the time! Mr. Gima was in his mid eighties then, so I suppose I was quite young!

"In 1955, as vice-captain of the Takushoku karate club, I took a group of students to my home and we gave a number of demonstrations in the area, including one in Miyako. Today, many people, both Japanese and from abroad, go to visit my former home. Tetsuo and his family don't mind. It is quite a big house, with eight bedrooms. I have happy memories of the house, it is beautiful, and from the garden you can see the Pacific Ocean. It isn't the house I was born in though, that was in Moshi too, but it was very old, made of wood of course, though simply too small for a family of ten.

"When I went home in the winter, being a student of karate at Takushoku, I used to practise. 'The secret of karate is daily training.'[12] I remember that I would climb up onto the roof of the house and launch

A group of friends stand before a gift shop in Moshi village, 1955. From left to right: Tanaka, Habu (with back to camera), Kanazawa, Okura.

myself off, practising the various jump kicks that karate has, especially *yoko-tobi-geri*. I could hold the correct position of the finished kick for a long time, which was highly beneficial, as normally it is over in a flash, and when I hit the ground my fall was broken by the deep snow we get in that part of Japan that used to drift up to the side of the house, blown by the wind. The hardest part of this training was actually getting out of the snow, as it was so deep, and because of the height I had fallen and the fact that I landed on my feet meant that I really did sink in deeply. When I went back to my home in the summer, I used to practise the same jumping kicks off rocks into the sea. It was good practice.

"Today, when I visit Tetsuo, I can relax. My brothers come around and we swap stories and catch up on family news. I like that. Tetsuo doesn't drink. I also go and see old friends. I always visit the cemetery where my parents, and Katsuo and Shin's ashes are buried.

"A number of students who enrolled in the karate club in 1952 with me, saw the four years through. Fujimoto became a manager of his family's cotton dyeing business, and he now holds the rank of 7th Dan JKA; Habu, I have spoken of before, and he is an 8th Dan of SKI; Terada is a 6th or 7th Dan, but does not now, to the best of my knowledge, belong to a karate association. He retired from business, and with his wife went to look after his aged mother. I understand he likes tending his garden. Kude I lost track of, and he never comes to reunions at Takushoku. Tatsunobu Fujito is vice-chancellor of Takushoku. Toriumi became a council member for the city of Shinjo, Yamagata Prefecture; Sagara went to Brazil teaching karate for the JKA and is now 7th or 8th Dan; Uryu also went to Brazil to teach karate and is a JKA 7th Dan, I think. He was recently involved in a car accident and broke both legs. I have noticed that many *karateka* seem to have car accidents. Maybe they drive as if they are doing karate? It is important to remember, for it is easily forgotten, that other drivers' reactions are not as fast as a *karateka*'s. Abe and Sata are now dead.

"Abe liked to drink. He challenged me to a drinking contest at university in our third year. He came from Shikoku, the island that lies between Honshu and Kyushu. One day he came to me and said, 'I understand you are a strong drinker?' I didn't know who could have told him this, and I replied that I didn't know whether I was strong or not. So he challenged me. I remember sitting in a small, wooden walled room of a drinking house and lining up the drinks before the competition. We both drank glasses of *sake* – Abe had one, then I had one, alternately – and because the owner of the house asked us to stop in case anything serious happened, we eventually called it a draw. Then we stood up and went to the doorway to put our shoes on. Abe bent down to tie his shoelaces and I heard, 'Oh! Errr...' and he collapsed. I picked him up, swung him over my shoulder, and carried him back to the dormitory. I've always considered that I won that contest really!"

III

THE JKA INSTRUCTORS' COURSE

Master Kanazawa continued: "My two principal professors at Takushoku were Teisuke Toyota, a very nice person, and Prof. Ichiko who, like me, came from north-east Honshu. He had a strong regional dialect and some students could not always understand him, but his lectures were very clear to me! I actually failed part of my finals, the English language exam, and expected to have to stay another year, but Ichiko asked me whether I wanted to stay, and when I said that I didn't, he arranged for me to re-sit the exam, which I did, and passed. I had trouble with English in those days, for we were required to learn difficult words necessary for business transactions, such as 'deduction' and 'exemption.' I liked the rest of the course, I enjoyed it, but the English …

"When I graduated from Takushoku with my B.A., it was decided that instead of working for Kanakan as originally planned, I would work for the Taiyo Fishery Company. I wanted to work for Taiyo because my family's business had dealings with the firm. I had no worries about a job, because it had all been arranged. But before I graduated, Nakayama *Sensei* came to Takushoku and asked me if I would like to join the JKA, as they were about to instigate an instructors' programme. I replied that I had to earn a living, that I was all set up, and that I wanted to help my family out. He said that I could do both, as I would have free time on the course, and that when my family's boats docked, I could check the cargo, and so on. Tokyo is situated on the shallow side of Tokyo Bay, and in those days only small coastal craft could use the docks, the larger ships putting-in to Yokohama, on the deeper part of the bay, which served the ocean going vessels. They were dredging Tokyo Bay when I was a student. 'Excellent,' I thought, I could have the best of both worlds, and I agreed to go to the JKA. However, the reality of events was somewhat

Master Masatoshi Nakayama

different. I should have learned from my seven days a week at Takushoku, because every morning, afternoon and evening, I had to do something at the JKA. This was a completely different story from that which

Nakayama *Sensei* had spun. I liked karate, so I wasn't angry. But during that year I did have trouble making ends meet. The JKA paid a very small salary, tiny. If I went out for a drink one evening with friends, that would be my month's salary gone!

"In those days karate wasn't well-known or understood by the general public in Japan, and in movies, the hero always knew judo and the villain always practised karate. The hero always threw the villain. As a student, I had had to earn money to survive and later, because the salary from the JKA was so meagre, I once again had to supplement any income with other work, as most students did, so I signed up as an extra in the movies and, later, as a bodyguard.

"I remember the film, *Hien Karate Uchi*, that was made about the history of the Takushoku karate club. The film was intended for general release and went all over Japan. I had a part in the film, as a *karateka*, so had many seniors – Nakayama, Nishiyama, Okazaki – but film actors played the major roles. The leading actors were Susumu Namishima and Hideo Takamatsu and the leading actress was Yumeji Tsukioka, who was very famous. That was in my last year at Takushoku. The film was a success and the film company produced two sequels and I was in both of them. I had lines to say too. It took a year to make the three films. The technicians always seemed to be at the Takushoku *dojo*. I believe the films have been placed on video as one of the celebrations to mark the centenary of Takushoku University. I attended the ceremony and it was a grand affair with one thousand guests. Emperor Akihito and his wife, Michiko, both attended. Afterwards, there were celebrations, to which another one thousand guests were invited. A number of prominent *karateka* in Europe, such as Enoeda, Asano, Ochi, Nagai and Miura were there.

"It was around this time, acting as an extra, that I became friends with Toshiro Mifune. [Mifune was one of Japan's leading actors, collaborating with director, Akira Kurosawa, in films such as *Drunken Angel, Stray Dog, Rashomon*, and, of course, *The Seven Samurai*]. Mifune played the lead role, a *judoka*, in *Sanshiro Sugata*, a character many actors have played, and I had to attack him. I acted in many films. I remember Mifune saying to me, 'Kanazawa *San*. Not too hard. This is just a film!' When we had the First SKI world championships [held at the National Olympic Stadium, Tokyo, on the 7th August, 1983], Mifune [then aged sixty-three] presented the awards [and a former Prime Minister, Zenko Suzuki, who I have mentioned before, gave an introductory speech].

"I also worked as a bodyguard for Daiei, the film company. There

Master Kanazawa, right, in a still from a karate film intended for cinema release

were two big movie companies at the time, Daiei and Shochiku. I worked as a bodyguard to the president, and was normally stationed at the entrance to the office. My job was to keep people away who were after donations. All the time people from charities were asking for money. When someone came to the office, I asked his or her name and business, and then passed this onto a girl who telephoned the president. It was normally a case of, 'The president is too busy.'

"Some people didn't take, 'The president is too busy,' very well. They actually became quite abusive, and a few of them threatened me.

I had a number of confrontations but never had to respond to violence, but I think it wasn't always just representatives from charities who wanted to see the president, and I suppose that was why I was there. Often these people would try and intimidate me. I was often worried about walking home at night because of these threats. I had to take special care, keep in lit streets, and go home by different routes. It wasn't a nice job, but I needed the money. I worked for Daiei for two years, on and off. I would have worked before, but early on in training I didn't have enough confidence to deal with the people I was expected to deal with.

"I remember when Rikidozan the famous sumo wrestler who became a wrestling promoter [and who was later murdered in a night club] came to see the president. [Funakoshi [1] mentions that he was told that Rikidozan had studied karate under Yokio Togawa, a former student of the master's].

"I also taught karate at the Daiei actors school for two years, during my last year at university and during my year on the JKA instructors' course. I enjoyed this work very much. I say I taught karate, but I actually schooled them in karate techniques for the movies, just what looked good on film. Whilst I was at the JKA, I was still acting as an extra in films. Sometimes I would go to the cinema to see myself, which was exciting, but in my mind I always had the expectation that I was better than I really was, and when I saw myself on the big screen I often felt ashamed."

The JKA was established as an educational body in 1955 under the Ministry of Education. Master Nishiyama recalled: "It was better for us [the JKA] at that time to become a public corporation as we could then come under the direction of the sports ministry which was also the Ministry of Education. My father, who was a lawyer, drew up the constitution and of course I had to contribute most of my time to it, writing and re-writing in order to get the JKA accepted as a corporation."[2] The number of karate 'styles' at that time was, according to Master Nakayama, 'about 200... And the public had no way of knowing who was qualified to teach and who was not. It was therefore our task to establish standards for instruction and register those standards with the Ministry of Education. So, under Master Funakoshi's guidance, I began formulating the Instructor Training Program. My feeling was that ranking should not be the only criteria for appointing instructors. It was even more important to teach them to teach others. They needed broad knowledge of other areas like physics, anatomy, psychology, management and so on. But this was a monumental task, and I had to

Master Funakoshi and Master Nakayama

have help and advice of the more senior students. So, along with me, significant contributions were made to the program by Motokuni Sugiura, Teruyuki Okazaki, Hidetaka Nishiyama and other senior instructors.'[3]

Master Kanazawa continued: "There operated a three tier intake system at the JKA. A student could complete the course in one year if he had been a captain or vice-captain of a strong Shotokan university *dojo*. Following Level A, the Level B course could be completed in two years, and the Level C in three years. All courses were full-time. I started at the JKA on the 1st April 1956. Because I had broken my shoulder during *kumite*, I was unable to grade to 3rd Dan at Takushoku as I had planned. I joined the JKA as a 2nd Dan and graded to *Sandan* the year I joined.

"Initially, there were only two students on this newly formed course, Takayuki Mikami and myself. [Mikami, at the time, was a twenty-two year old Japanese literature graduate from Tokyo's Hosei University. He had come from a farming community in Niigata Prefecture, where at school he had studied judo and kendo, but he had become totally absorbed in karate once at Hosei, almost to the detriment of his academic studies. Kimio Ito had recommended Mikami for the JKA Instructors' Course]. Later, Eiji Takaura joined us as a third student. He had attended Chiba Engineering University. He had a patent and had no money worries. I don't think he practises karate anymore.

"Training on the instructors' course was not quite as hard as the

Master Kimio Ito

training at Takushoku, but we spent more time practising, and the science of karate was explained to us. We trained every day again. Mikami and I became good friends and we shared digs near the JKA.

"When we got to the *dojo* in the morning, we changed in the small dressing room, no lights, and then cleaned the *dojo*. I never minded cleaning the *dojo*, running up and down as we did, it was good physical training, but the real benefit, I found, was that it cleansed the mind. Washing the floor, to me, was like polishing a diamond. After cleaning the floor, while it dried, we practised on the *makiwara* that were located outside. I think there were three *makiwara* – one for each of us! Then we trained, had a small lunch away from the *dojo* – we could never afford a decent meal – came back and had more training. Then we'd have dinner and go back to the *dojo* for evening practice. Because we were student instructors, we also had to teach three lessons a day. We trained in karate and we taught karate, that's all we did, day in, day out. We tried our best to improve, not only for ourselves, but also for the JKA. [Master Mikami referred to exactly this point in an interview, noting that: 'We felt lots of responsibility to make the program a success'[4]].

"The JKA *honbu* in those days was based at 13, 1-Chome Yotsuya, Shinjuku-ku, and was an old and somewhat dilapidated and shaky building in a busy part of Tokyo a few minutes walk from Yotsuya railway station, and was owned by a film company [Kataoke Film Centre]. The *dojo* had been the film preview room and had a highly polished dark wooden floor and wooden panel walls. Sometimes, we'd break part of the floor when we came down hard with *fumikomi*. It wasn't large ['about 50 or 60 square metres only, so we were limited'[2]]. In fact, now I come to think of it, it was still occasionally used as a preview room when we were there.

"The ceiling was high. The Japanese flag was hung at the front of the *dojo* as did the *dojo kun*. There was also a full-length mirror mounted on a wall, as was a wooden rectangular frame, inside of which, on wooden tablets, *nafuda*, were the names of successful students. There was also, in large *kanji*, 'The ultimate aim of the art of karate lies not in victory or defeat, but in the perfection of the character of its participants,' which, of course, was one of Funakoshi's maxims. The stairs in the small office, to the left as you entered the building, led up to the film company's cutting room. Masatomo Takagi was always there, as was his female secretary. [Takagi, who, it is believed, was forty-three years of age at the time, referred to himself as 'the gatekeeper at the JKA'[5]].

"Takagi was a very nice man, honest and kind. He looked after everyone, especially, later, the foreign students, who liked him. It was Takagi who acquired the JKA *dojo*, and things may have been very different if Nakayama hadn't approached him for help.

Takagi had been a founder member of the Takushoku karate club and was one of Funakoshi's first students. During the war, Takagi had been a journalist working in China. When the war was over, he went to

Masatomo Takagi

live in Hiroshima, continuing working in his profession. Nakayama went to see him and asked for advice on how to get the JKA started. One of Takagi's classmates at university was the younger brother of a film producer, and Takagi went to see him and said that after the devastation

Master Kanazawa and Masatomo Takagi in Sapporo City – Tokyo, mid to late 1950s.

of the war, not only did the country need rebuilding, but so did the people, and as it was the young people who would do the rebuilding, karate would give them the resolve to accomplish the task. The producer agreed, and that's how we acquired the *dojo*.

"That *dojo* was very nice, I thought. There was a good atmosphere there. Takagi was happy with the *dojo* and proud for what it stood for. I remember one day a group of representatives arrived from different universities – Waseda, Chuo, Keio, Takushoku, Senshu – and some of them said that the *dojo* was too small and began criticizing it. Takagi was offended after all the work he had put in. I think he said that it was big enough for us, and I don't think some people, from other universities, came any more.

"Our main instructors at the JKA were Nakayama, Nishiyama and Okazaki. Funakoshi *Sensei*, who was technical adviser, would also come and watch and explain things. He was a very quiet person, a very modest and reserved person, very private. He never wore a *gi* at the JKA though, always a kimono. When I was at Takushoku, he wore a *gi*. He wore his *gi* quite tight and short in the arms and legs, and he actually looked rather like a beginner today, which is very strange. He wore his black belt like we do today, and not tied in such a fashion that the knot lies on the left side, as he did when he came from Okinawa. Funakoshi took this idea from Kano, because he respected him greatly, as I have said,

Master Nakayama and Master Funakoshi

and because he wanted karate to be a Japanese martial art. We never really knew, we could not really understand, what Funakoshi wanted from us, what he required us to do. He was a very old man at the time [eighty-eight in 1956]. Nakayama was close to Funakoshi I think, and was like him in a number of ways. They both thought about education. Funakoshi had been a teacher on Okinawa for more than thirty years, and Nakayama was a university lecturer [later professor], and they were both concerned for the next generation – not just Japanese, but worldwide. They wanted peace, and they both considered karate a means of spreading it.

"It was whilst I was at the JKA instructors' course that Funakoshi's autobiography, *Karate-Do Ichiro* [*Karate-Do: My Way of Life*], was published. I thought that was a nice book, it was real rather than trying to convey a myth. It contained good advice and ideals to aim for. I wanted to be like Funakoshi *Sensei*.

"Even today, all these years on, there are many *karateka* on Okinawa who do not recognize Shotokan. I remember Mr. Tatetsu who came from Okinawa to study at Takushoku and then proceeded onto the JKA instructors' course. When he went back to Okinawa in the 1960s, he took Funakoshi's karate with him, but he wasn't recognized. He had a lot of trouble; he told me that. They said that Funakoshi *Sensei's* karate was sport karate, not real karate. It is a difficult question. I do not think it is true because Funakoshi didn't like sport, but I suppose he let it happen. I don't know if he could have stopped it though. He was old. Funakoshi *Sensei* taught good form to encourage a good spirit.

"There were also other seniors who taught at the JKA as well, *karateka* like Arai and Yanase from Takushoku; Obata, Mochizuki and Akiro Yamamoto from Keio; Kamata, Noguchi and one other I can't remember from Waseda; another Yamamoto, Kimio Ito, and someone I cannot remember, from Hosei. We had the advantage of many seniors coming to give us their knowledge and their training methods.

"Nakayama *Sensei*, although quietly spoken and of gentle demeanour, was self-assured and a very hard instructor. As well as being the JKA's Chief Instructor, he was also Director of Physical Education at Takushoku. He wanted the JKA instructors' programme to be a success, and as we were the first crop, we had to be the best they could make us. Nakayama taught *kihon*, combination drills, and a great deal of one-step sparring. Strange as it may seem, we were expected to work on the *kata* in our own time. *Kata* was seen as a subject for personal study, for personal development. Our improved basics were made manifest in the forms."

Master Mikami recalled of the JKA lessons: "Hard, yes, I would say so. We were the first ones, and this was a new thing. Everyone was curious, so the seniors [such as Nishiyama, Taiji Kase and Masaru Sakamoto] would come to visit our classes, especially at lunchtime. There would be ten of them and the three of us, and we would have to fight the whole line. Yes, it was hard!"[6]

Master Kanazawa continued: "The Instructors' Course involved more than simply hard training in Shotokan; we knew about that, we could

Gichin Funakoshi oversees training at the Yatsuya *dojo* in 1956. To the founder's right is Masatomo Takagi, and to his left, standing, Master Kimio Ito. Note the black American sitting front row, three from Funakoshi's left, and the two youngsters to Takagi's side.

do that. The purpose of the course was also to broaden our understanding. A number of notable *karateka* from other styles, such as Gogen Yamaguchi, came to give lectures, master classes, as did *kobudoka* from Okinawa to teach traditional weaponry. We also had a number of distinguished academics in diverse fields to give us lectures in kinesthenics, physics, psychology, biology, and so on. Nakayama *Sensei* was the brain behind this. To get karate truly established, he knew it would have to have a firm and rational base. Teaching the SAC [Strategic Air Command] personnel had shown him a direction for karate's expansion.

"We also had to learn how to instruct. Sometimes, a senior would join the lesson, not only to see how we were teaching, but to learn what it was like to be taught again at a basic level." Nishiyama recalled this very point: "In the beginning, I used to go to every class. I would put on a white belt and stand in the back of the class and see if I could learn *oi-zuki* or *zenkutsu-dachi*. I would try and make my mind just like a beginner. If the instructor's voice didn't have enough punch or he didn't explain things enough, I would make a note and would bring it up in instruction training. This was very difficult for the instructors of course,

Master Kanazawa

but also for me. I had to attend every session – beginner, intermediate and advanced. It was very tiring. But it was also a great help to me in seeing how the beginners were receiving their instruction.'[2]

Master Kanazawa continued: "The hardest part of the instructors' course was when we were visited by university teams from other styles who came for *kumite*. Many people were curious as to what Shotokan were doing. I particularly remember Mr. Shogo Ujita from Wakayama Prefecture, southern Honshu, and his Goju-ryu team of six students. Only Goju-ryu operated in Wakayama, which is about four hundred kilometres from Tokyo, and Ujita was second in seniority to Gogen Yamaguchi *Sensei*. That *kumite* was hard. They were very good. I did not fight. I was asked to sit and watch. I knew something serious was going on when the seniors began to arrive and get changed. Okazaki was there, so was Yanase and Irie. Okazaki *Sensei* I thought was best, then the Goju-ryu *karateka*, then the other JKA seniors. That was my opinion. I was just sitting there waiting, waiting, and I wanted to fight but I wasn't given a chance; I don't know why.

"Two years later, Asai, who had come to the JKA for instructor training, and myself, were scheduled to travel to [a here unmentioned] prefecture where a particular style dominated, to perform a demonstration. We were told [by persons not here mentioned] that if we went into this prefecture, we wouldn't come out again. It was about territory, about power. It was serious, very serious. Asai and I said that that was okay, we'd go anyway, but Nakayama put a stop to it."

Master Mikami, concerning these inter-style contests, recalled: "They wanted to see what was going on. What was the JKA doing in this special program? Other groups and styles came to the JKA to challenge us. That was tough, free-sparring with no referee."[6] [We were] "always under pressure, since *karateka* from outside wanted to check out the kind of training we were receiving. People from the Kansai area would send their team – which was very strong – to practice with us and 'test' us. One time they sent ten *karateka* ... and there were only three of us! And this was a regular occurrence. Sometimes the Takushoku University karate coach would send all their senior students over to 'train' with us. Really, it was a kind of competition. Many people came to test the three JKA instructors."[7]

Master Kanazawa continued: "Mikami was an *oi-zuki* specialist, especially at *chudan* level. He was very strong and very fast. Takaura was also strong, but he had no particular technical strengths. The three of us used to get up to all sorts of mischief. For example, we used to kick roads signs with *mawashi-geri*. They were the right height for practising *jodan* kicks, and *jodan mawashi-geri* became by favourite technique! When the police arrived, we used to run for it, but Takaura used to get caught because he was built solidly and wasn't very fast.

"I remember going to Shizuoka to Minoru Mochizuki *Sensei's dojo.* [It was Mochizuki's son, Hiroo, who first taught karate, Yoseikan karate, in Europe in 1956]. Mochizuki was a famous *judoka* and *aikidoka* [and had trained in karate for a short while under Gichin Funakoshi at Jigaro Kano's request]. At Mochizuki's Shunpukan, a very famous *dojo*, they taught a number of martial arts, including karate, and the karate section was considering affiliating to the JKA, or perhaps they just had, I can't remember now, but they wanted to know what we were like as they had a greater heritage than us. They wanted to practise *kumite*, and I paired-up with Tetsuji Murakami, who was instructing there, and who was shortly to come to the JKA for a few months before being invited to France [in 1958 by Henri Plee. Murakami was a 3rd Dan in Yoseikan karate and, after his training at the JKA, a JKA 1st Dan]. It was decided not to punch or kick *jodan*, which I wasn't that happy about, because, as I say, that excluded my favourite technique, not to say techniques, and *chudan* techniques were agreed upon. They then said that opponents should wear kendo armour, which is made from wooden slats, to protect ourselves, but I said that wasn't sufficient to stop a blow, for karate blows penetrate, but they didn't understand about karate blows, and they were unprepared for what happened. Before I started, I asked, 'Shall I do kick[s] *chudan*?' He [Murakami] said, 'Okay *chudan*, okay.' I said, 'No! If I kick I break, *Sensei.*' 'No, no, impossible; strong body, no break' [Murakami replied]. We started *kumite*. Bang! Break! Therefore he [Murakami] very unhappy.'[8]

"At the end of a JKA class, we used to say, with purpose, the *dojo kun*, expounding the five basic principles of karate: – character, sincerity, effort, etiquette and self-control:

Hitotsu! Jinkaku kansei ni tsutomuru koto!

Hitotsu! Makoto no michi o mamoru koto!

Hitotsu! Doryoku no seishin o yashinau koto!

Hitotsu! Reigi o omonzuru koto!

Hitotsu! Kekki no yu o imashimuru koto!

In Japan today, we at SKI still recite the *dojo kun* every day out of respect for Funakoshi, Nakayama and Takagi. I do not insist on it in other countries, it is up to them if they wish to say it or not, but it does

Master Kanazawa performing an *otoshi-empi-uchi* during a demonstration at a kendo *dojo* near Kodansha – 1957.

offer sound advice and can instill good karate values and social manners.

"Sometimes, a strong individual would come to the JKA and make a challenge. I remember Mr. Kon, from Meiji University, an extremely powerful *judoka*, who practised Shito-ryu. He held a Dan grade in each

Masters Kanazawa and Mikami practising *ippon-kumite*

art. He was taller than me and specialized in *jodan mawashi-geri*. He came to the headquarters and wanted to challenge, and I was put against him. I won, but after that we became friends and he joined the JKA.

"We finished the JKA instructors' course on the 31st March, 1957, and I became a full-time instructor for the JKA. I was teaching at the *honbu dojo,* but I was also travelling a lot, all over Japan really, especially to the universities like Kanto and Taisho, Nippon Dental School, Showa

Medical School, and so on, that didn't have established karate clubs. I went to many universities. My youngest brother, Hideo, started the karate club at Showa, and I used to teach there regularly. I also used to teach for companies. I was happy because I was doing what I loved. I was training every day, a full-time instructor.

"A few weeks after I'd graduated from the JKA instructors' course, Funakoshi *Sensei* died [on 26th April]. He passed away in hospital; his heart had given way. Everyone was very sad, and a cloud seemed to hang over the *dojo*. His early students, like Nakayama and Takagi were damaged deeply by his passing. But Funakoshi taught that we must have a strong spirit, and that is what we tried to do.

"Mikami went to the Philippines [in August, 1957] not long after he'd finished on the Instructors' Course. [The president of the Philippine delegation to the Asian Games, which were held in Japan that year, trained at the JKA and became friends with Mikami]. Originally, he was to go to [the Far East University Karate Club] Manila, for two or three months, but his contract was extended to nearly one year [to May, 1958]. Then he came back to instruct at the JKA for some five years, until he was sent to the United States by the JKA. [Initially to Kansas City, Missouri, then shortly afterwards to Los Angeles, California, and then to New Orleans, Louisiana, where he is currently based]. I remember when some friends and I said farewell to him at the railway station. We performed a special dance for him on the railway tracks and prevented the train departing. It was just youthful high spirits really. The police came and said we must move. 'In just a minute,' I replied, 'we've nearly finished.' 'No! Now! You are holding the train up!' a policeman insisted. I pushed this policeman and he fell down. It was a stupid thing to do, and the police were correct. Then more policemen came and we all made a run for it. I went to the railway station and got onto a train, another train, back to Tokyo. But the train didn't move! A message had come through that they were looking for us and that the trains had to be searched. I sat down and when the police came, they said I was to go with them. An American in the carriage who I had never met, to my utter astonishment said that the police had got the wrong man, because he had done it! They took his name and details, said that they would be in touch, and then left. I asked the American why he had helped me and brought trouble upon himself, to which he replied, 'I'm off home to the States tomorrow!'"

IV

THE JKA CHAMPIONSHIPS

The first JKA All-Japan Championships were held on Monday, 28th October 1957 [some writers have noted June, 1957], at the Tokyo Metropolitan Gymnasium, the premier centre of its kind in Japan at that time, in front of some eight thousand spectators. Careful preparation had ensured that this event was to be a Shotokan showcase, and most of the spectators were *karateka* from various styles wishing to see not only the JKA standard, but also how such a large competition would fair.

Master Nakayama had struggled with the idea of karate's promotion. Many of the Old Boys refused to be associated with the sporting contest, believing it degraded the art, and were confident that it was the very antithesis of what Gichin Funakoshi had stood for. Nakayama and the JKA saw things differently however, believing that competition would launch Shotokan's next evolutionary step. Kendo and judo were flourishing as sports, and, so the reasoning went, unless karate could establish sensible rules, rise above the reality of the *kokangeiko*, it would never be accepted and have a major following. Nakayama recalled that the *kokangeiko*, "in essence were the first 'free-style' matches. Two members of opposing clubs would face each other, scream a loud *kiai* ... and charge in ... the blows were not pulled at all and the *sempai* of the group would have to leap in and separate them. This was rarely necessary however, as usually it was all over very quickly – some men had broken jaws and noses and teeth knocked out; some had their ears practically ripped off their heads whilst others would be lying temporarily paralyzed from kicks."[1] Clearly this state of affairs could not continue.

However, Master Nishiyama painted, perhaps, a slightly different picture: "Mostly, karate was in the universities and we exchanged training, not only with the Shotokan group, but with any style. Afterwards we were all great friends. Of course we didn't have any rules for *kumite* so there was no control, but afterwards we all got together, everything

The Tokyo Metropolitan Gymnasium at the time of the fourth JKA Championships – 1960.

was fine, and I still have many friends from these competitions."[2]

Nakayama continued: "After much thought and observation of the rules and competitions of other sports, I experimented with and finally developed a code of rules and conduct and also a fighting style that allowed *karateka* to attack and counter-attack each other freely and powerfully – but with controlled technique that would spare them from injury."[1]

With regard to *kata* competition, Nakayama reflected: "My greatest concern at that time was to ensure that karate, if given a sporting aspect, would not lose its essence as an art. I therefore worked very hard on designing *kata* competition, and I based the rules on the rules of skating and gymnastics competitions [dancing and diving have also been recorded]. My only hope was to preserve the essence of Karate-do as an art of self-defense and self-denial, and to prevent the excitement of sparring from transforming karate into a mere sport."[3] However, a 'can of worms' may be said to have been opened. Six years later, in the 1963 JKA championship programme, it was noted in the opening line of 'Karate Match' that, "To defeat an opponent in competition is not the final purpose of karate training;"[4] and as short a time as eight years after the first JKA Championships, Nakayama was writing that "a problem has arisen with free-style sparring which cannot be ignored. We must consider it now lest the true meaning of Karate-do be endangered."[5] The notion that *real* karate might be lost in competition haunted Nakayama until his death.

THE JKA CHAMPIONSHIPS

Mr. Shuji Masutani, President of the JKA

Master Nishiyama recalled: "The Japan Karate Association devoted over five years to devise a working set of tournament rules. During the period they not only discussed the theoretical problems, but members of the committee were in the *dojo* ... clad in their karate *gi* ... experimenting and exploring what was possible and [searching for] practical standards to formulate for both *kumite* and *kata* contests."[6] "The JKA contest rules, comprising three chapters and sixteen articles, were completed in August of 1956."[7] Selected paragraphs from the official rules have been published.[24]

Master Kanazawa continued: "It was decided in the first year of the championships that a contestant could either enter the *kata* or the *kumite*. Only black-belts could compete. I decided to enter the *kumite*, though I thought I would have to withdraw before the event, for I had broken my right hand sparring in preparation for the championships four days before. I actually broke a bone when I fell on it sparring with a senior who insisted on *kumite* when I was tired. I went to the doctor's and he said I shouldn't compete, and the JKA said I shouldn't either. Contrary to what people might expect, I was actually very happy with this decision, because it meant that I could rest. I wouldn't have to train for a few days.

"Then, two days before the championships, my mother made an unannounced trip to Tokyo. 'Oh! This is a surprise!' I exclaimed, when I answered my front door, 'Why have you come?' 'To see my son compete,' she replied. Then I explained to her that I wouldn't be competing because I had broken my hand and that I had been advised not to enter for fear of further damage. My hand, wrist and forearm were bandaged and were supported by a sling, so it was pretty obvious. 'It is impossible for me to enter,' I explained, and then my mother said something I shall never forget. 'I am sorry,' she replied, almost apologetically, 'I thought that karate used the whole body. You have injured one hand – what is wrong with the rest of your body? You still have two feet and another hand. Why can't you fight? Karate is a martial art isn't it? I must be confused about karate.' Of course I knew all this, but it was her tone and the way she reasoned it that made me appreciate that perhaps I'd given in too easily. I then explained that I had withdrawn from the competition and the rules, as I understood them, forbade me to enter at this late date. My mother was very disappointed.

"So, I went back to the JKA and explained things to Mr. Takagi, the secretary, and I told him about my mother. Takagi had trained with Funakoshi long before the Pacific War, but I don't think he practised much, if at all, at the time. He was the JKA's administrator. ['He was shortish, round-faced, with the air of an affable, good-natured businessman'[8]]. He listened intently, and I think was very impressed with my mother's opinion. Takagi said that if the doctor agreed, gave me the all clear, then it would be allowed. When I went to the doctor, my mother insisted that she accompany me, and we persuaded him. So,

I could compete, but I couldn't rest.

"The night before the competition, in a dream, I worked out what I would do, the strategy that I would employ. I think that in the back of my mind was a story involving my sister many years before. When Shin was about thirteen or fourteen, she walked from Omoto to Moshi, about four kilometres, with an open basket on her back with fish in it. Along the path, she saw two foxes. One fox stared at her, and then trotted off down the path, stopped, waited for Shin to come closer, and then trotted off again, but it always kept just ahead of my sister. The other fox ran off and remained unseen. This first fox's stopping and starting, happened quite a few times, and Shin became quite transfixed by the creature's strange behaviour. When she got close to home, she realized that the basket she had been carrying was much lighter, and when she examined it she found it was empty. Then she knew why the fox had behaved as it had, for it had acted as a decoy whilst the other fox stole the fish from the basket right off Shin's back.

"I had used dreams to help me since I discovered the benefits in childhood, and I found that I could sort out all sorts of problems this way. Later, when I was with the JKA, I remember dreaming two *kata* for a student who had no arms. I dreamed them and woke myself up in the middle of the night and wrote them down. If I hadn't woken myself up, I'd have forgotten them by the morning. I called the *kata Daichi Shodan* and *Daichi Nidan*. They were kicking *kata*, and contained nearly all the Shotokan kicks in them – *mae-geri*, *kekomi*, *kesageri*, *ushiro-geri*, *mawashi-geri*, and maybe *mikazuki-geri* and *keage*, I can't recall now. I also taught kicking *kata* to two Japanese boys who had thalidomide, no arms, who became black-belts.

"The contest area at the JKA championships was eight metres square, and then there was another metre or so around the perimeter, and the whole space was raised up about one metre off the floor. There was a middle line in the centre, marked off with white tape, as were the two contestant lines, behind which bouts commenced, and the referee's line. Officials sat by tables on two sides, with one of these sides having the cups to be won displayed for all to see. Despite my strategy of using my broken hand as a feint, I was still very nervous that first bout. I just wanted to show my mother her son winning once. I won the first match and I was very surprised, and when I went into the second round, I was very relaxed, because I'd done what I had set out to achieve. I won the second round and the third round. All these rounds I won with kicking techniques. I couldn't afford to clash and risk getting my hand injured

The Tokyo Metropolitan Gymnasium at the commencement of a JKA championship.

further, so my favourite techniques came into their own that day. I did use my injured hand as a feint however, for even though my opponents probably knew I wasn't going to strike with it, they weren't sure, and the speed at which the feint was employed deflected their attention momentarily, and this was sufficient for me to score. The doctor examined my hand after every bout. My grandmother was in attendance too, and she implored, 'Enough! Enough!' after the third round. I can remember that clearly. I had to explain to her that if I won a bout it was a competition rule that I had to move into the next round. I realized at this stage that the competition was down to the quarter-finals [which means the initial pool was sixty-four or about that number with byes or fight-offs], there were only eight competitors left, and I naturally wanted to see how far I could go.

"I won the 4th Round match, also with kick, and then in the semi-finals I met Mr. Nakamura, the captain of the karate club at Hosei University. Nakamura had studied my form very carefully, and he knew that if a distance was created between us then he stood no chance, for my kicks were superior to his. Therefore, his tactic was to get in close to prevent me from kicking, or, if I did kick, there would be no point scored because of the distance. A stalemate situation developed. He always wanted to close the distance and I always wanted to create distance – a very interesting scenario. At last, he delivered a kick, a *mae-geri*, and I jumped up and scored with a strike to the head. The techniques were simultaneous I thought, though, in truth, Nakamura's kick didn't score. Mister Miyata, the referee, said that Nakamura had scored a *wazari*, a half-point.

"Now, as the audience was mostly composed of *karateka*, they didn't like what they had seen and they shouted and threw things. 'No! No!' they chanted, 'Kanazawa hasn't lost!' I bowed out and came down from the raised competition area. A senior said to me, 'Why are you coming down? Get back up there! Get back up!' So, I did. This was very serious, remember the championships were to be a shining example of the JKA and they wanted to get it right, so they called a meeting, referee and judges, and decided to cancel the result and have a re-match. I think this is the only time this has ever happened at the JKA championships. So, Nakamura and I faced-up for a second time, and on this occasion justice, at least as I saw it, was done and I beat him with a *chudan mae-geri*. I was in the final!

"Standing on my marker in the finals, the referee was to my side, and four judges sat, each in one corner, with white and red flags. In one corner, off the raised area, an arbitrator sat high up in a tennis umpire-like chair so that he could see the whole proceedings. There was also a starter, a timer and recorder, just as there is today. My opponent in the final was Katsunori Tsuyama, who was captain of the karate club at Takushoku, and All Japan University Champion. Tsuyama, who is now professor of karate at Takushoku, had a *jodan mawashi-geri* that was unblockable. It was so fast you could barely see it. I knew I had to work out a strategy to beat him, especially as I couldn't use one of my hands. He was always successful against opponents because when he kicked, they tried to avoid by moving backwards or sidewards, but the *mawashi-geri* was just too fast. Even if you were quick enough to block with two hands spread apart, it was very difficult, and he was upon you. So, what should I do? Instead of moving backwards or sidewards, I decided to step forwards as he kicked, but I had to be fast, really fast, otherwise I might catch the knee or shin in the head, and at that speed that would have meant hospital at the very least.

"We both got up, bowed to each other, and then to Nakayama *Sensei* who was the referee. The atmosphere was very tense, as one might imagine, but not just between Tsuyama and myself, for the audience seemed to generate a real intensity and you could feel it in the air like static. Here was my chance to make history, to be the first JKA *kumite*

The 1957 JKA individual *kumite* final. Master Kanazawa, in the process of a throw, steps in to avoid Katsunori Tsuyama's famous *mawashi-geri*.

champion. I knew it would not be long before his *jodan mawashi-geri* was let loose, and I was prepared when his left leg came up. I stepped forward and *teisho'd* his left shoulder with my left hand. Tsuyama was very surprised, I don't think he had ever experienced this before, and as I stepped in with my left leg, I threw him.

"Then we faced each other again. I immediately attacked *mae-geri* and then straight away *mawashi-geri* – I had no intention of letting him get over the shock of being thrown. I knew that if I launched just one attack he'd block it, because he had really good reactions, so I used the *mae-geri* to open him up for the roundhouse-kick. Sure enough, he blocked the *chudan mae-geri*, which was really a feint, a half-kick, and he followed his *gedan-barai* up with a *chudan gyaku-zuki*, but I had jumped up slightly and performed a *chudan mawashi-geri* with the other leg, and his punch didn't score, but my kick did. Nakayama's hand went up. '*Ippon!*' I had scored a full-point.

"Then we began a third time. I knew from experience that I could try the combination again, and there would be a possibility of success. The second time, immediately after the first time, is often successful, a third time, never. So, I thought I'd give the combination another go, and I launched a *mae-geri* intended as a feint and then jumped higher to score another *ippon* with *jodan mawashi-geri*. [This contest was no doubt the beginning of a series of events that led one magazine to write of Master Kanazawa, twenty-six years later, that 'he is known by many in the JKA as the most skillful fighter of all time...'[9]].

"Shoji took the *kata* title with a very nice *Unsu*. So, Takushoku Old Boys had taken both titles, and this made us, and the university, very pleased. In those early competitions there were no team events." Later, Master Nakayama wrote that, "It was Mr. Hiroshi Shoji who fascinated the spectators fully by his excellent performance, full of power and beauty,"[10] and Master Nishiyama described Shoji's performance of this complex form as "flawless."[11]

Master Kanazawa continued: "I couldn't really believe that I'd won to be honest. I was naturally very proud, as was my family, and I remember being presented with my trophy and certificate from Mr. Shuji Masutani, president of the JKA. Masutani didn't practise karate, he was a Member of Parliament."

Master Nakayama recalled of the first JKA championships, that they "were most impressive – attack and counter-attack with rapid, powerful, well-controlled technique. The *kata* contestants displayed quick, beautiful movements. Both the fighting and the *kata* left the audience impressed. Not one contestant was injured in the free-style fighting. The new matches were a great success."[12] Certainly, he wrote that the championships "turned into a scene of wild enthusiasm and excitement because of the wonderful performances staged by the karate players."[10] Then, in another interview, Nakayama noted: "The first one [championships] was a huge success. Before that, karate had been seen as a type of physical education, and also a defence art; but after competition began, it also became widespread as a sport – it became much more popular."[13]

The immediate interest in the new sport was evident in that the finals were shown in a collection of news items in cinemas, few people having television in Japan at that time. However, Master Kanazawa did not recall ever seeing these films.

It is interesting to note that Master Hironori Ohtsuka commented that 1957 was also the first year that Wado-ryu held their first sporting contest.[14] From what Nakayama has said, it is likely that this followed the JKA championships, and in 1962 the Japan Karate Federation was formed by leaders of the Shotokan, Wado-ryu, Goju-ryu and Shito-ryu styles.

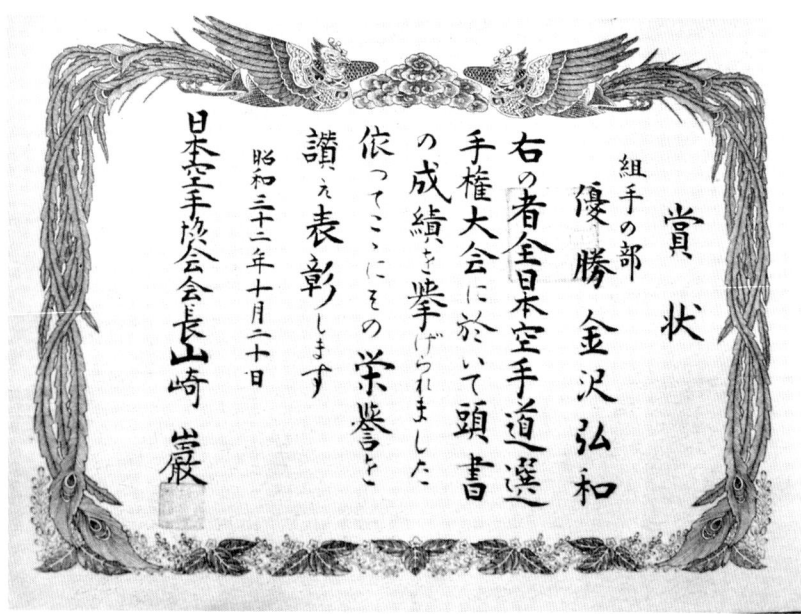

The 1st JKA championship title certificate for *kumite* – 20th October, 1957

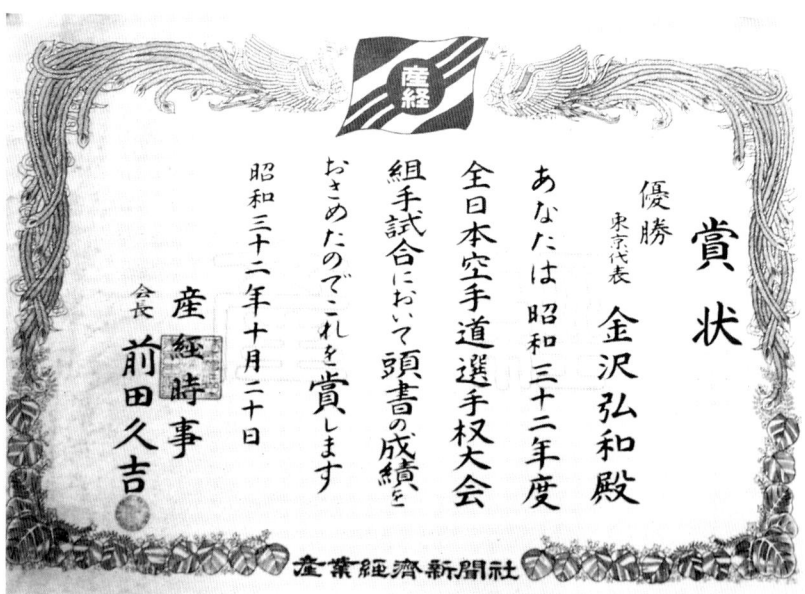

The 1st JKA championship title certificate for *kumite*, presented by the president of the Sankei-Jiji Newspaper – 20th October, 1957.

Master Kanazawa with his mother, shortly after he won the 1st JKA *kumite* title.

Master Kanazawa continued: "The following year, the 1958 championships, one could enter both the *kata* and the *kumite* events. I entered both and was fortunate enough to win both [thus becoming the first JKA Grand Champion. This achievement has only been repeated a further five times since: Takayuki Mikami (1959), Hiroshi Shirai (1962), Hiroshi Ochi (1966), Masaaki Ueki (1968) and Masao Kagawa (1985)]. In direct contrast to the 1957 finals, where everything my opponents did seemed to happen in slow motion, all the competitions seemed lightning fast in 1958! However, I was in peak form that year and I had great confidence, though I was very happy to win! I used dreams and daydreams to help me once again, and I kept largely to a diet of fish and vegetables, though once a week I had meat, because I felt I needed a different type of protein. I also made sure that I had no caffeine.

"In the *kumite* finals I met my friend Mr. Mikami. We knew each other very well of course, and it was difficult for either of us to score. Mikami was generally punching and I was generally kicking. Mikami rushed in and I countered. Nakayama, the referee once again, called a half-point, but Nishiyama ran in and the two talked, and it was decided

From left to right: Habu, Mrs. Habu, Kanazawa's cousin (mother's brother's daughter) Suzue Hatakeyama, Kanazawa's mother, and the master – Tokyo, 1958, before the 1958 JKA Championships.

that the strikes had been simultaneous. I had a tremendous following in the crowd, who were chanting, 'Kanazawa! Kanazawa!' Boys and girls, men and women, they were all cheering me on. There was a lot of applauding, and it was very exciting. One girl gave me a flower, but I don't think Mr. Nishiyama approved of this. 'This is Budo, not a party!' was his comment.

"Then I launched a kick at Mikami, but I didn't score. At the end of the match, there was no winner, so there was an extension of one minute, I think, but at the end of that, neither of us was up, and so there was a second one-minute extension. There were four extensions in all, during which neither of us scored, and at the end of the fourth it was decided to call the match a draw." This was the only tie in the history of the JKA championships.

Master Takayuki Mikami recalled: "That was the hardest match I ever fought in my life! We knew each other so well, what techniques and strategies would be used. There was never a point, because if I started a charge, he made one at the same time. When he moved, I moved.

[The match, having reached its fourth extension of time]: "We were both exhausted. I just wanted to quit and give the whole thing up. I didn't care about trophies any more. But my family was watching, and all those people in the audience. I couldn't give up. And then I realized that he (Kanazawa) was thinking the same way. So I said, why should I give up?"[15]

Master Kanazawa catches Master Mikami with a *chudan mawashi-geri* in the 1958 or 1959 JKA Championships.

In another interview, Mikami noted: "We pushed ourselves mentally to the maximum in order to get a chance to score. I knew that if I attempted to penetrate his guard, he would be waiting for me and immediately counter-attack. Mister Kanazawa's range is longer than mine by at least three inches, so it was very hard finding a way to break through his tight guard. After a while we were both extremely tired, physically and mentally. I didn't care any more about winning, or getting a trophy. I just wanted to lie down on the floor! However, our spirits kept feeding us with new energy. Also, I received some 'outside energy' from the audience ... you see, my home town is Nigata, far away from Tokyo, and all my family had come to see me. Also many friends from my college karate club were there; everyone was expecting to see the best from me. So this took me to my limits. Kanazawa is a strong fighter and it seemed as though I would have to move twice as fast as him if I wanted to score. On that day, the spirit of those people who were supporting me gave me 'big power.' Otherwise, I would have quit or even lost the match."[16]

In yet another interview, Mikami reiterated: "There was a lot of mental strategy and tactics involved. We knew each other's technique, so it was a matter of mental strength."[17]

Master Kanazawa continued: "That final was draining. At that level, you have to give everything – mind, body and spirit – and think of

Master Kanazawa performing his winning *Sochin kata* at the JKA Championships – 1958.

nothing else. There is nothing else in the world, and your world, or your opponents, can end in a fraction of a second. Karate is very dangerous. You live on the tip of your nerves. Mikami was the best tournament

Master Kanazawa is presented with a diploma by Zentaro Kosaka, the government foreign affairs minister, and a *karateka*, who later became President of the JKA – 1958.

fighter I ever encountered." In another interview Master Kanazawa noted: "He was small, but he had extremely fast movement and superb timing. Very fast punching, kicking ... all at the same time; no hesitation between his techniques."[18]

Master Kanazawa continued: "In the *kata* final, I wanted to perform *Gankaku* which was my favourite form, I really liked it, but Nakayama *Sensei* insisted that I should perform *Sochin* as I was better at it, and so I did. Fortunately I won, so I was happy, but I wasn't very pleased at all when Nakayama *Sensei* first told me to change. In the early rounds you were asked to perform a basic *kata*. Two contestants would come up, bow, and perform the required *kata*, and the judges would raise a red or white flag depending on whom they thought had given the best performance. The final, which had eight contestants, was judged using the point system however. There were seven judges, and the highest and lowest scores were taken away and the remaining five scores were added to give a total score. Mikami came second and took the silver medal that year [every year between 1958 and 1962 Mikami took medals], but I can't remember who came third, it was a long time ago, though Asai was there, so was Shoji, I think. Toru Iwaizumi did a nice *kata*. Iwaizumi has since changed his name to Yamaguchi."

Five years later, we have what are believed to be Kanazawa's first published view on *kata* in the West: "The basic forms and movements are practiced without any opponent. By just imagining the opponent a

Master Mikami receives his trophy – 1958

karateist can fulfill every form practiced. It is very important, therefore, that while practicing the karateist put his whole heart, soul, and mind into the form. Then the purpose of defeating an opponent becomes complete."[19]

Master Kanazawa continued: "I did have a film of the 1958 finals, but I lent it to an English student from the London *dojo* in 1965 and

Master Kanazawa and Master Mikami with their JKA trophies – 1958

never got it back. I would very much like to see that again, but I understand the student didn't train for long, so I suppose it's gone forever. [This student has now been identified from photographs].

"I must be honest and say that a few seniors did not take my winning kindly. I don't know if it was jealousy or what. Perhaps they thought I was big headed, but I wasn't; that's simply not in my nature.

"In 1958 there was also a karate competition held between eastern Japan and western Japan. There were many good Shotokan players there. I won the *kumite* individual title, beating Masashiro Sato, but in the final of the team event I lost to Asai. There were only two teams, as the best fighters from the north and south had been selected. The team event was seen as more important than the individual title, and all I could say to the northern team was, 'Sorry.'

"I wasn't happy about the outcome of the 1959 JKA individual *kumite* final, when Mikami and I met again. No, I wasn't happy at all. I take nothing away from Mr. Mikami though, for what follows wasn't his

The 2nd JKA championship title certificate for *kata* – 4th October, 1958

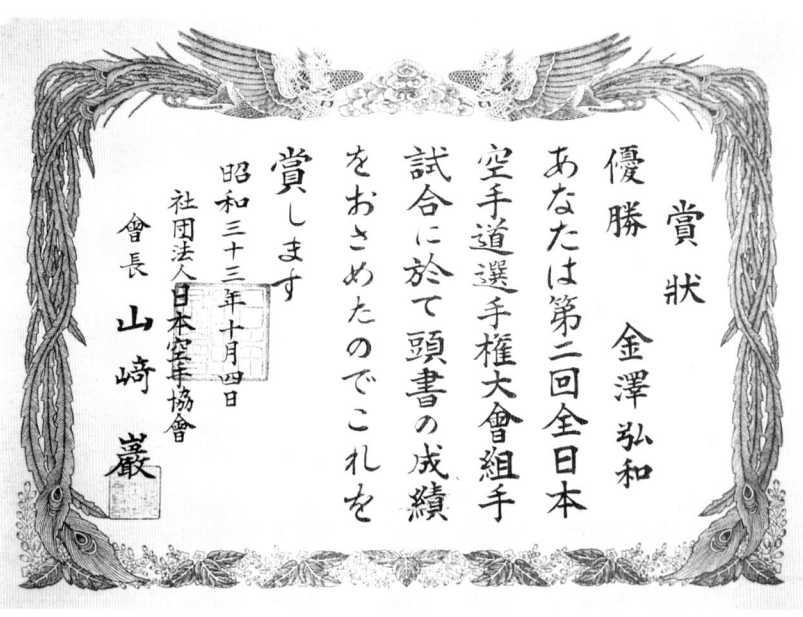

The 2nd JKA championship title certificate for *kumite* – 4th October, 1958

THE JKA CHAMPIONSHIPS

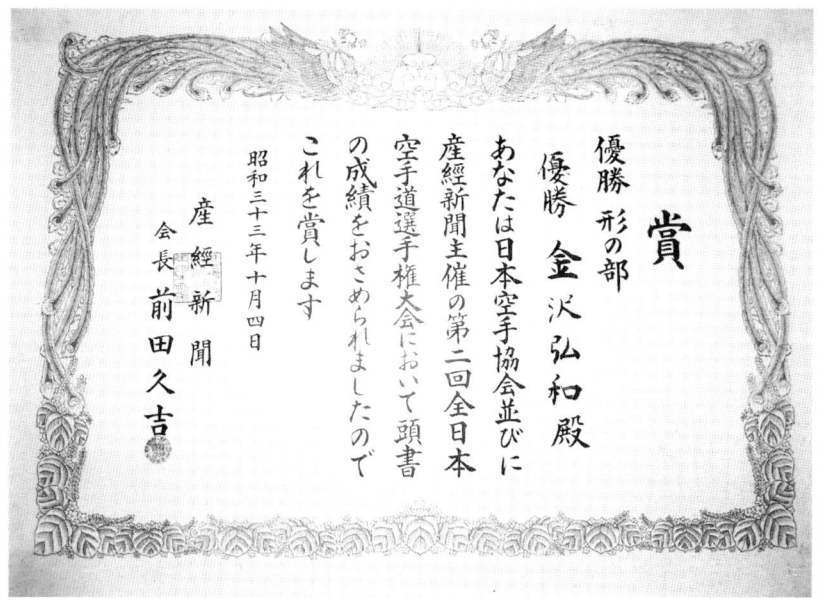

The 2nd JKA championship title certificate for *kata*, presented by the president of the Sankei-Jiji Newspaper – 4th October, 1958.

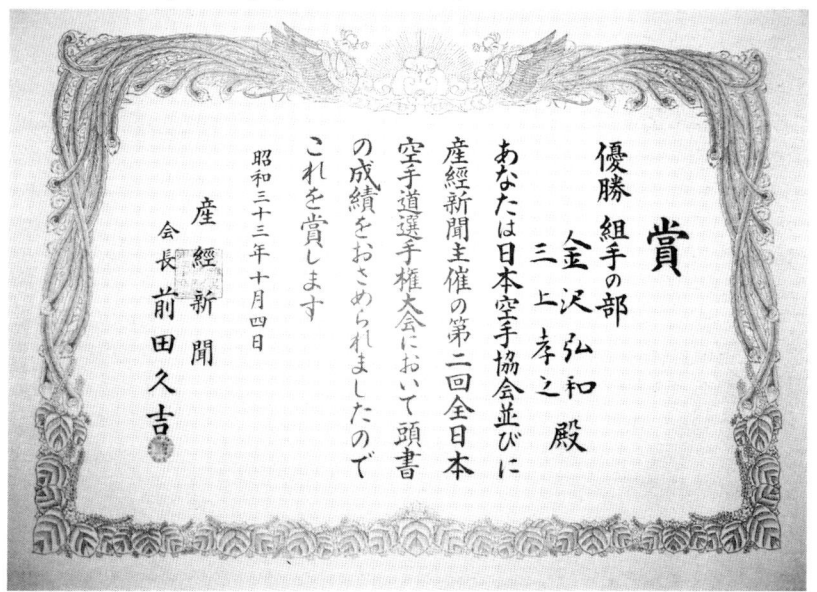

The 2nd JKA championship title certificate for *kumite*, shared with Takayuki Mikami, presented by the president of Sankei-Jiji Newspaper – 4th October, 1958.

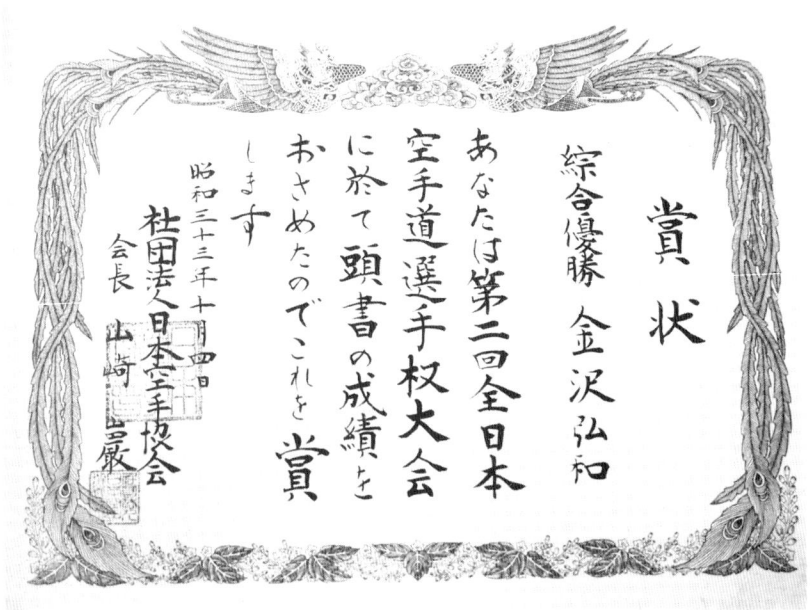

The 2nd JKA championship title – Grand Champion certificate – 4th October, 1958.

fault in any way, and must not detract from his achievement. In the final, Mikami attacked *chudan oi-zuki,* and at the same time I punched him *jodan*. Nakayama, the referee yet again, said that Mikami had scored and that I had missed, but I had caught Mikami's teeth lightly because his teeth marks were on my knuckles. I was very unhappy, but I bowed out and Mikami won. The following day, Mr. Shoji approached Mr. Nakayama and reported that my punch had made contact. 'No! No!' Nakayama replied. I was standing next to Shoji and I showed Nakayama *Sensei* the teeth marks. 'Oh!' Nakayama exclaimed, 'Not enough focus!' I bowed and said, '*Oss.*' If I'd knocked Mikami's teeth out I would have been disqualified."

Mikami, in an interview, was asked whether anything different happened in the 1959 final compared to the 1958 final. He replied: "No, I don't think so, I was just lucky. My body moved without conscious thought. There was no planning, just concentration."[17]

Master Kanazawa continued: "Mikami also took first place in the *kata* that year performing *Kanku-sho*. I took the silver medal with *Sochin*. I can't remember who came third, either Shoji or Asai, I think.

"The following week, I had my 4th Dan grading and I was very

Master Kanazawa in May, 1959. Note the *makiwara* by the master's left arm and the JKA lapel badge.

happy, because I knew I would partner Mikami during the freestyle. I wanted to put right what had happened at the championships. Many people came to that grading because they knew that both Mikami and I

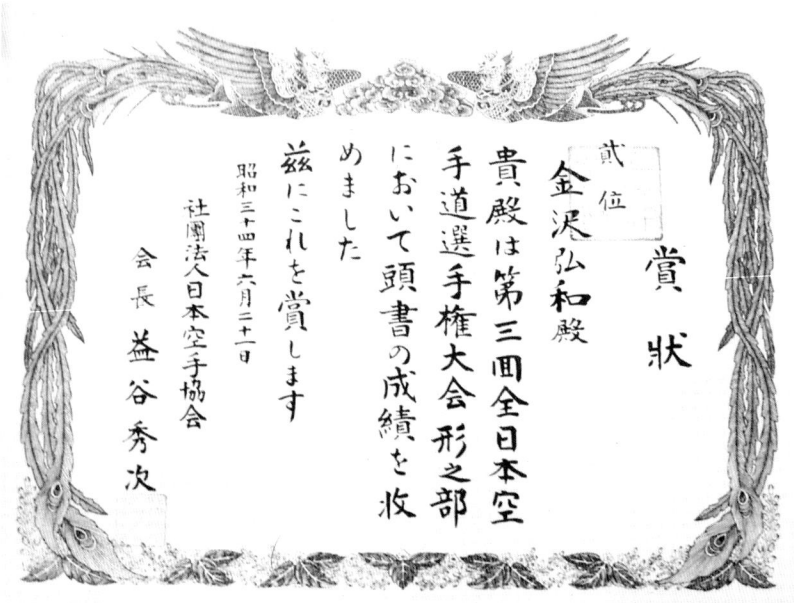

A 3rd JKA championships' certificate – Kanazawa, 2nd place in *kata* – 21st June, 1959.

were Grand Champions, and some knew how I must have been feeling about the recent championship result. There were so many people at the grading that some were watching through the windows from outside. After *kihon* and *kata*, I was excited, and very expectant at the prospect of the *kumite*. Then, Nakayama *Sensei* stood up and said that everybody understood that both examinees were good at *kumite* because of their tournament results; therefore it would not be necessary to perform *kumite* as part of the grading. I was really disappointed!

"After the 1959 final, I started to think more deeply about what karate was about. I learned many things, not least that my opponent in the arena did not appear to be my only concern. I realized that speed was a problem, because the referee didn't always see the techniques. Greater control was necessary.

"The [June] 1960 championships were attended by many people ['some 10,000'[20]]. Sato, from Sendai, took the *kumite* title, and Shoji the *kata* title again. In the quarter-finals I fought Sato. I scored first with *chudan gyaku-zuki*, then I did the same technique again, but I didn't score. Then Sato scored against me with *chudan oi-zuki* after throwing a nice *ashi-barai* feint.

The flag that was presented to Master Kanazawa for winning three consecutive JKA titles.

"In 1961 and 1962 I was instructing in Hawaii, so I didn't take part in the championships [in 1961, Asai took the individual *kumite* title beating Shirai; Enoeda and Mikami were joint third, and Mikami took the individual *kata* title. In 1962, Hiroshi Shirai took both titles, meeting Enoeda in the *kumite* final].

"There were many good competitors at the championships in the early years, before the Olympic Games, people like those I've spoken about and also many others like [T.] Miyaki. I remember in the Kyushu Championships when another good competitor, Ken Nakaya, clashed with a senior *karateka* now living abroad and this instructor broke Nakaya's neck – *batan*! It was nobody's fault; it was just an accident. [The author wrote to the instructor concerned hoping for a comment on the incident, but was not favoured with a reply. As the issue is reported here by a third party, the author has decided not to reveal the name of the said instructor]. Nakaya was much lighter than most other competitors, only about eight stone, and was also quite a bit smaller, just over five foot, and he clashed with someone heavier, taller, senior, and much more powerful. At the time, Nakaya was in his mid twenties, and he has been in hospital ever since, for more than thirty-five years now, unable to move his body below his neck. I make a point of visiting him every year, and give him money that I've earned from teaching karate. It is the right thing to do. It could have easily happened to any one of us. It was very sad, heartbreaking, because he was about to be married, and he told his intended to make a new life for herself. It is strange though, because for all these years he has lain in hospital never able to move anything, but now he can move his hand, not his fingers, just his hand. [Many of the *karateka* mentioned by Master Kanazawa, to date, including Nakaya, can be seen in the JKA promotional films of the time. These films are to be strongly recommended].

"The JKA made many films during the 1950s and 1960s. In, *Karate-Do: Part 2 – Self-Defense,* I acted as a partner because I was a junior. I assisted Okazaki [defence from the sitting position, and defence against a pistol], Nishiyama [defence against a club attack] and Nakayama [defence against a surprise attack (along with Okazaki)]. These films had been planned by Nakayama and were filmed on 8mm in the famous Chinzanso gardens in Tokyo. [The film in question was supervised by Asao Fujii, photographed by Yoshiyuki Hanazawa, and is of $8^{3}/_{4}$ minutes duration]. We filmed quite early on in the morning and the grass was wet, so some people encountered difficulties and you can see the odd little slip, the odd slow move that became faster [Master Kanazawa made reference to Yasuhiko Mochizuki's *Kanku-sho,* when the *bo-uke* is shown quite quickly, as a possible example of this, for Kanazawa attended the filming].

"The JKA also did a series [*Techniques of Karate* – Global Films, Tokyo] in six parts. These were filmed at Chinzanso too. Many good *karateka* were featured performing different *kata*. I was shown in the fourth film performing *Enpi*. I remember getting to the *teisho-kosa-uke,* near the end, coming towards the camera and someone shouted something and I stopped. I then carried on, but you can see the break in the film – very bad editing! One thing that we performed differently in those days was the first *kiai* point. Today, when in *kiba-dachi* and performing a *jodan haishu-uke,* the move prior to the first *kiai*, we come up with an upward movement with the right arm and at the same time we move the left foot forty-five degrees, and perform *kataashi-dachi*. On the film, you can see that we kept the left foot stationary when coming up, and brought the right arm over and down.

"Also, the ground wasn't anything like as even as it looked, and that is why you sometimes see the odd wobble in a *kata* performance." [The *karateka* featured performing *kata* in these films are: Film 3: Nakaya – *Heian Shodan*; Asai – *Heian Nidan*; Sugiura – *Heian Sandan*; Shoji – *Heian Yondan*; Iwaizumi – *Heian Godan*. Film 4: Sugiura – *Tekki Shodan*; Shirai -*Tekki Nidan*; Nakayama – *Tekki Sandan*; Kanazawa –

Master Kanazawa, jumping over an opponent's club, is in the process of performing a *yoko-tobi-geri*, in a Japanese self-defence film. Note Master Keinosuke Enoeda in the background.

Enpi; Enoeda – *Jitte*; Mori – *Chinte*; Kase – *Jion*. Film 5: Enoeda – *Bassai-Dai*; Iwaizumi – *Bassai-Sho*; Ueki – *Gankaku*; Mikami – *Hangetsu*. Film 6: Nakaya – *Kanku-Dai*; Mikami – *Kanku-Sho*; Shirai – *Sochin*; Asai – *Nijushiho*; Nakayama – *Unsu*].

"The *kata* haven't changed at all really since those films were taken, just the odd little movement is different. For example, in *Kanku-dai*, when I was taught the foot movements prior to performing the two *keage/uraken* techniques, before performing the *shuto-uke* in *kokutsu-dachi*

Master Kanazawa (standing, centre) at a seminar held in an old Buddhist temple in Kamakura – 1957–1959.

[see moves 10 and 52 in Kanazawa's, *Shotokan Karate International Kata: Vol. 1*], you moved the left foot up first on both occasions before kicking with the right leg. Today, I believe the JKA make a half-step with the left foot, as before, on the first move, but miss this out on the second move and come straight through and kick with the right leg. In SKI, we have changed too, but do the exact opposite to the JKA. I thought it much more desirable when in a shorter stance [move 10] to come straight through and kick, and that a half-step would be best when the stance was full [move 51].

"Nakaya [who demonstrated *Kanku-Dai* in the films above], and others come to that, would also perform their *shuto-uke* differently. The old way, the way I was taught, was not to straighten the reaction arm, but to block from the hips, keeping the arms in position of the previous *shuto-uke*, and then moving that way and swapping them around at the last moment, as one landed in the next *kokutsu-dachi*. This is very good, it is better for *kumite*, but it is more advanced. Later, it was changed for the purposes of educating the body, physical education, in that when the reaction arm is straight, it helps bring the whole body into play, and helps to keep the hips square until the last instant.

"In *Heian Sandan*, after the three *fumikomi/empi-uke/uraken*

Master Kanazawa teaching at a seminar for students of the Japan Travelling Agency and Showa Medical University – 1958–1960.

techniques, the *chudan tate-shuto-uke* was performed slowly, but Mr. Motokuni Sugiura performed it more quickly at the time and didn't arc, so I don't know what happened. Today, many people, including those in SKI, perform this move slowly and arc the *tate shuto-uke* [see move 18 in Kanazawa's, *Shotokan Karate International Kata: Vol. 1*]. Now that Mr. Sugiura has taken over as Chief Instructor of the JKA, people don't put the *fumikomi* in after the first *kiai* in *Heian Godan* [see move 11 in Kanazawa's, *Shotokan Karate International Kata: Vol. 1*] and near the end of *Kanku-Dai* after the *Tekki*-like sequence [see move 60 in Kanazawa's, *Shotokan Karate International Kata: Vol. 1*], as I have mentioned before. These are the old ways of doing these moves.

"Nakayama didn't know all the *kata* that are practised today, and when a detailed question arose about one of those *kata*, he used to ask me to speak to Mr. Sugiura, who was from the Asia University in Tokyo.

"In *gyaku uchi-uke*, such as in *Heian Nidan*, we didn't use to pull the *zenkutsu-dachi* back [see moves 13 & 15 in Kanazawa's, *Shotokan Karate International Kata: Vol. 1*] – we did in *Bassai-dai* [see moves 3 & 7 in Kanazawa's, *Shotokan Karate International Kata: Vol. 1*] – whereas today, many people do. I think that it is best to pull back; there is a better feeling in the hips. It's the block that makes the front foot come back; it is a natural movement, a natural block.

"In the JKA *Jiin*, the opening *kosa-uke*, the two *kosa-uke* after the kicks and punches after the first *kiai* point, and the single *kosa-uke* after the punches and kick following on from the last *tettsui/kiba-dachi* sequence are the same. The *gedan-barai* follows the leg that is forward. In SKI, we perform the opening movement the same as the JKA, but I changed around the position of the arms on the remaining three *kosa-uke*, because I felt that it was more natural. Therefore, on these changed *kosa-uke*, the *uchi-uke* corresponds to the leg that is forward [see moves 1, 16, 21, 30 in Kanazawa's, *Shotokan Karate International Kata: Vol. 1*].

"In *Kanku-sho* we used to *kiai* on the jump [see move 25 in Kanazawa's, *Shotokan Karate International Kata: Vol. II*] [this can be seen in Mochizuki's performance noted above] but it was changed to the last *oi-zuki*. Mochizuki is senior to me, and today is with Shoto Domonkai. The *kiai* should be on the jump. In that *kata,* the first *kiai* is a positive *kiai*, a punch, an outward release of destructive energy; the second *kiai* must be negative, an inward feeling of energy, and therefore it cannot be on a punch, but either a block or a jump.

"The idea of positive and negative, Ying and Yang, opposites but unity, is very poorly understood in Shotokan." Master Kanazawa has elaborated upon this point elsewhere: "It is a question of balance ... *Kiba-dachi* is very solid and strong, this is good for stability. However, *shiko-dachi* allows for a little bit more flexibility for moving and it is important to have both options for the student. We need this flexibility I think. Not just in the stances, but also in how our own minds work ... It is important to understand that even in strength there are many different kinds ... Which has the more strength, a rock or water? When I think of these stances, I feel that the *shiko-dachi* is more about [being] internal, bringing things in, gathering *ki*. *Kiba-dachi* is more external, and pushing away, expanding ... [oneself]."[21]

Master Kanazawa continued: "In *Tekki Sandan*, Funakoshi and Nakayama performed a slightly different *kata*, and we were taught this version on the JKA Instructors' Course. Nakayama later changed it to that which is practised today, though there are a number of variations. [If the reader watches the fourth film mentioned above, the old version of the *kata* may be seen. The main variation is the sequence from the third (sometimes fourth) movement, and is too involved to go into here].

"Many people today perform a high leg-lift on the fourth move of *Gankaku* to show flexibility and balance skill, but the lift was minimal when I learned it. [Master Kanazawa demonstrated the leg lift as in the sixth move of the *kata Gankaku-sho*]. No! No! You mustn't change the

Teaching Showa Medical University students – 1959/1960

weight ratio. People who lift their legs right up change the weight ratio. There are other ways to practise flexibility and balance without misusing the *kata*. [The leg lifts in *Gankaku* and *Gankaku-Sho* are now performed by the master in the same fashion, but move 4 in Kanazawa's, *Shotokan Karate International Kata: Vol. II* may lead readers to assume that the way indicated is the incorrect method no longer recommended by the master. Whilst it is true that the leg is much higher in this photograph than that now evident, the weight ratio is actually correct].

"Also in *Gankaku*, I used to perform the *jodan shuto-uchi* in *zenkutsu-dachi* just like the JKA still do. I changed this for SKI and perform the *shuto-uchi* in *kiba-dachi* [see move 33 in Kanazawa's, *Shotokan Karate International Kata: Vol. II*] and then move into the *zenkutsu-dachi* when I perform the *tate empi-uchi* [move 34]. I think that this is best; otherwise there is no room for the elbow strike.

"In *Hangetsu* the opening blocking and punching in *hangetsu-dachi* sequence used to be performed a little faster and more smoothly. It is a question of breathing.

"The old way, the original way of performing the move where today two *yoko-geri-kekomi* can be seen in *Nijushiho* [see Film 6 above], was simply to lift the leg up and perform a *fumikomi*, and to keep the arm out. I'm not sure, but I believe it may have been Mr. Okazaki who put those kicks in, and this was approved by the JKA, and it is what we do in SKI [see moves 7 & 9 in Kanazawa's, *Shotokan Karate International Kata: Vol. II*]. In one of the earlier films [*Karate-Do: Part 2 – Self-Defense*], Mr. Fasajiro Takagi from Keio University is seen performing *Nijushiho* without the *kekomi*. [This is an interesting film because a number of differences, both of technique and timing, occur in the *kata* compared to today's JKA and SKI version. One of the most obvious, and intriguing, is the final sequence, for whereas Takagi performed the *awase-zuki* with speed and the *mawashi-kake-uke/awase teisho-zuki* likewise with speed (see moves 23 & 24 in Kanazawa's, *Shotokan Karate International Kata: Vol. II*), the JKA and SKI perform the last move slowly. Also, Takagi put the *kiai* in on the *awase teisho-zuki*, whereas it is customary today to *kiai* on the *awase-zuki*]. This Mr. Takagi, who is dead now, was one-time FAJKO general secretary, and he also gave an introductory speech at the first SKI world championships.

"I also used to teach *mawashi-geri* in *Enpi*, instead of the *fumikomi* after the *age-zuki*, because there were no *mawashi-geri* in *kata*. I later reverted to the original *fumikomi*, however." [Of the alterations Master Kanazawa has made to JKA *kata*, this is probably the most famous. He taught the *mawashi-geri* in Great Britain when he was resident between 1965 and 1968, and a few of his students of the time still practise that way]. Master Kanazawa has elaborated upon this point too, elsewhere: "[But] it was not the *mawashi-geri* that was important. I had noticed that we used the kick a lot in *jiyu-kumite*, and we also practised it many times in *kihon*, so I wondered why it was not used in our *kata*? I wanted to have a *kata* where a student could use the kick. But it was more important that the student realized that they *could* use this kick. I know people were saying things about me, that I was changing the *kata*, and that this was a bad thing. But you know in olden days this happened all the time. *Kata* must be of some help to a student, not something separate from the rest of their training. Funakoshi *Sensei* did the same thing when he changed the *mae-geri* to *yoko-geri* in the *Heian kata*. Of course one should not change the *kata* just for the sake of changing it, but if the reason is good then in my opinion it's okay."[21]

Master Kanazawa continued: "I changed the names of *Gojushiho-Dai* and *Gojushiho-Sho* around, because I believe that is the correct way. The creator of these *kata* said that *Dai* was the form with three consecutive techniques – *ryu-un-no-uke, osae-haito-uke* and *shihon nukite*. *Gojushiho-Sho* is the form with *ippon-nukite*.

"Also, Funakoshi never taught *jodan* punches in *kata*, at least not at Takushoku. Today, there is a single *jodan-zuki* in *Jiin*, but

Master Kanazawa (centre) before training on the seashore at Miyako City – 1960.

Funakoshi didn't teach that *kata*. Even the *sanbon-zuki* in *Jion* are all *chudan*. I believe *chudan-zuki* were given priority to teach good form – shoulders down, hips down – for when punching *jodan*, form can easily go. [Funakoshi devised the *Taikyoku*, of which there were originally three. All the lunge punches in *Taikyoku Nidan* are *jodan* and *Taikyoku Sandan* contains six *jodan oi-zuki*. However, even universities where *Taikyoku Shodan* was taught, notably Waseda and Chuo, the remaining two *kata* appear not to have been practised]. Personally, I do not teach *Taikyoku* [*Shodan*], but some SKI *dojo* do. It is a *kata* that is very kind to beginners. My opinion is that beginners need *Heian Shodan* as their first *kata*; they need something more mentally and more spiritually demanding from the outset in my view. [*Taikyoku Shodan* has only one type of stance (excluding the opening/closing *hachiji-dachi/heiko-dachi*), one type of block, and one type of punch, whereas *Heian Shodan* has three types of stance, three types of block (two of which can be readily interpreted as strikes), one type of punch and one type of strike].

"*Unsu* is an interesting example of change. The stance before the jump, originally used to be *kiba-dachi*, then it changed to *kokutsu-dachi* and then it became *fudo-dachi*. We in SKI have kept *kokutsu-dachi* [see move 33 in Kanazawa's, Shotokan Karate International Kata: Vol. II].

Masters Okazaki, Nakayama, Kanazawa and Kobayashi with an American general

Originally it was changed because older people had difficulty. I think *kokutsu-dachi* is kinder on the knees."

"In the JKA, they perform the opening two moves from the *kata Wankan* in *kokutsu-dachi*, whereas in SKI we perform the opening sequence so: we step over diagonally with the right foot, then bring the left foot forward into *neko-ashi dachi*, then we bring the left foot across horizontally, and move the right foot forward into *neko-ashi dachi*. I do this not so that it is easier to end up on the same spot as one started, but because I wanted to have the feeling of Funakoshi's *kokotsu-dachi*, which was much shorter, in this *kata*. You will note that the distance covered in the first two movements corresponds to a modern *kokutsu-dachi*."

Perhaps the most notable difference observable in a single *kata* by virtue of these early 1960's films, other than *Tekki Sandan*, whilst allowing for individual variation, is in Master Nakayama's performance of *Unsu*. After performing *jodan haito-uchi* in *zenkutsu-dachi*, and then kicking *mae-geri*, the *soto ude-uke* are performed in *zenkutsu-dachi* rather than on one leg, as they are widely practised today [see moves

18c & 20c in Kanazawa's, *Shotokan Karate International Kata: Vol. II*]. Also, half-way through the *kata*, after the *gedan oi-zuki*, the next two techniques are widely understood to be, and practised as, *gedan-zuki* [moves 23 & 24], as one shifts direction back and forth. On these two moves, Nakayama clearly performs *gedan-barai* and not punches, bringing the fists, one at a time, up to the shoulders. Perhaps they are intended as sliding-block punches? These little technical points are interesting historically, and have been included for reader enjoyment and further involvement. The issue will not be laboured however, for one is always cognizant of Master Nishiyama's words: "Ninety-nine percent of *karateka* misunderstand *kata*. They only set the outside movements which are irrelevant."[22]

Master Kanazawa continued: "But I think that *kata* has changed, and been influenced by competition and what judges look for, what they can see. It has become more like gymnastics I think. It has lost much of its meaning. Now, people perform *kata* and they all look alike. No, this is not *kata*! Also, 'in *kata* competitions I can see an over-emphasis on [the] 'magnificence' of the *kata*,'[23] but this is just theatre. I am fearful too, that if karate becomes an Olympic sport, then *karateka* will be free to devise their own *kata* for competition purposes. Some countries are experimenting with this already. One country I know in the Middle East has devised its own *kata* in anticipation! No, they don't understand.

"Today, Shotokan karate in general is not what it was when I was a student. Modern karate has become more recreational. The summer schools are now designed so that students enjoy them, but fifty years ago they were a hell to be endured and then overcome; something not enjoyable at the time, but which gave great reward afterwards. I don't know what the summer schools in Japan give students these days. The black-belt grade forty or fifty years ago was not the same as today's. Then, spirit and strength were the most important elements, but today technique is the important thing. I believe the real karate level has dropped because of the lack of hard training in basics. Tournament karate has got a lot to answer for. In SKI I try and keep the standard up, but students don't like repetition of basics, they want variety. I have found this to be a worldwide problem. Funakoshi *Sensei* noted this too, so it may be a trend.

"In 1959 or 1960, I took part in the photograph sessions, along with Mr. Nishiyama and Mr. Okazaki, for the book, *Karate: The Art of 'Empty-Hand' Fighting*, by Nishiyama and [Richard C.] Brown, which was published by Tuttle in 1960. That was a good book I think, very influential. I was also featured in Nakayama's, *Dynamic Karate* (Kodansha, 1966). Some of those photographs were taken before I went to Hawaii, but the majority were taken after I had come back and before I went to England. That book was the result of Nakayama's scientific studies into karate, and as such was the first of its kind. I thought that book was very good too, and it certainly helped karate get established in the West.

"I taught the occasional western student at the Yotsuya *dojo*. I remember one army officer, a US general, a very big man aged over fifty, who Takagi asked me to teach privately. I recall that we would sometimes go out for a meal after training and eat western style. I enjoyed the meals very much, but I had great difficulty using a knife and fork, because I always ate with chopsticks of course. I remember that this man had such rank and influence that the military police, usually a law unto themselves, wouldn't touch him.

"Another American I taught was Donn Draeger. He wrote a number of books on karate with Nakayama *Sensei*, which helped spread the word of the JKA. [There were six such books under the *Practical Karate* heading and published by Tuttle, so: (1) *Fundamentals* (1963), (2) *Against the Unarmed Assailant* (1963), (3) *Against Multiple Unarmed Assailants* (1964), (4) *Against Armed Assailants* (1964), (5) *For Women* (1965), and (6) *In Special Situations* (1966)]. He was an influential person, a pioneer in a way, who took his martial arts extremely seriously. He was a very nice man, a very serious man, very private, and had the bearing of a Japanese samurai."[Draeger had been a major in the US Marine Corps, and settled in Japan in the mid fifties after seeing much service in the Far East. He was primarily a *judoka*, but had studied aikido, *jodo* and sword, among other arts. He died on the 21st October, 1982, aged sixty].

V

JKA CHIEF INSTRUCTOR TO HAWAII

Master Kanazawa continued: "Nakayama *Sensei* said I had to go to Hawaii, but I wasn't so sure I really wanted to. However, on the 22nd January, 1961, a large group of friends came to bid me farewell as I caught the Japan Air Lines over-night [3,400 mile] flight from Haneda to Honolulu, the capital of the Hawaiian Islands, as the JKA representative. It was my first time away from Japan. I climbed the stairs to the plane, and when I got to the top, I turned, smiled, and waved, but I was full of mixed emotions. I was to be totally on my own in a strange country. I was sent to Hawaii as a kind of troubleshooter, to sort things out, though I didn't know this at the time. Someone from Waseda University, a past graduate, an Old Boy, had taught there for a year, and a problem had apparently arisen, I can't remember what it was now, but the JKA had been asked to send an instructor over. We knew that Harada was in Brazil and had set up Karate-Do Shotokan Brazileo [see [10, 11]] and I thought that he had stayed in Hawaii before settling in Sao Paulo. I now understand this is incorrect.

"Anyway, it was my first time on an aeroplane too. 'My happiness was interrupted [though] when I wanted to be seated in the cabin. [The] stewardess told me that my ticket was for the tourist class, and the entrance I [had] entered was of the first-class. I didn't know there were two class[es of] air travellers, and found that the Association was not so rich [as] to buy me the first-class ticket. She explained that the entrance for tourist class passengers was at the tail side. But how could I show myself up again to the people, to descend the trap where I came from, walk down far away to the tail of the plane and ... [climb] the trap belonging to the tourist class. I asked her to let me go to my seat through the inside passage. She let me go inside. The ... [journey] to reach my place was felt as ... [far away as the Sahara desert]'[1] (i.e. the master was embarrassed).

Takushoku students see Master Kanazawa off from Haneda Airport – January, 1961.

"I sat next to two Canadian women. After a few hours, we got chatting, but my English wasn't very good. I became quite alarmed because they casually said that one of their favourite Japanese dishes was *ochinko*, which means 'testicles.' Thankfully, their Japanese wasn't very good, and they actually meant o*shinko*, or 'pickles'. I hadn't really done any preparation for Hawaii, and I should have brushed up on my English; it was a mistake. On the aeroplane, for example, I didn't know how to ask where the toilet was, and as I'd had a beer at the airport I needed to go."

The Hawaiian Islands, covering an area of some 6,423 square miles, in 1960 had a population of 632,772, and only the year before had been accepted as the 50th State of the USA. Master Kanazawa was to be based on the diamond-shaped island of Oahu, formed as a result of two immense volcanoes that had eroded to form two rugged parallel mountain ranges with peaks to just over four thousand feet. Covering 604 square miles, the islanders relied mainly on the production of sugar and pineapples, and on tourism for their income. Oahu's capital, a modern city, stretched ten miles along the shore and four miles inland. In 1960, Honolulu had a population of 294,179.

Ohshima, a graduate and former captain of the Waseda University karate club, had settled in Los Angeles as an exchange student in 1955,

Master Kanazawa and Masakuni Murakami at Haneda Airport on the evening of Kanazawa's departure for Hawaii – January, 1961. Murakami is a Member of the Japanese Parliament and President of the Shotokan Karate-Do International Federation.

when ranked 3rd Dan, and had begun teaching Shotokan at the Konko Shinto Church the following year, forming the Southern California Karate Association shortly afterwards. Ohshima is regarded as the pioneer of Shotokan in the USA and was considered an exceptional *karateka* in Japan. In 1959, Hiroshi Orito, another exchange student from Keio University and a Shotokan 2nd Dan, started teaching karate in New York.

Nishiyama and Brown, only a few months before Kanazawa's arrival, had noted that: "It became apparent a few years ago that the growing interest which many foreigners, both in Japan and abroad, had begun to show in karate was more than a superficial attraction to the exotic."[2] How true this was, and four months after Master Kanazawa had come to Hawaii, Master Okazaki arrived in Philadelphia, and in the summer Master Nishiyama returned and based himself in Los Angeles, forming the American Amateur Karate Federation in November that year. Later, Master YutakaYaguchi ['a very stern and tough teacher'[3]] arrived to act as his assistant. Master Mikami, who, after returning from the Philippines in 1958, arrived in Kansas City, Missouri, in 1963. The almost

Master Kanazawa on his arrival in Honolulu – January, 1961. Td Hara is to the master's left, James Tompkinson, to the master's right.

evangelical approach of the JKA had started in earnest, and it was the beginning of a movement that would spread throughout the entire world.

Master Kanazawa continued: "That first day in Honolulu was full of surprises and it didn't go very well at all. When I arrived at Honolulu airport I went through customs and met a problem. 'Where are you going to?' an immigration official asked. I replied that I was staying in Honolulu. 'But your case is marked to go to Los Angeles,' he said. I had mistakenly picked up a suitcase that was identical to mine. I tried to explain that there had been an error, but my English wasn't very good. Fortunately, the president of the karate club I was going to was also the chief immigration officer, and of course they were expecting me. Luckily, I also got my case back at the airport.

"There were quite a few people [about thirty] waiting to greet me from the Butoku Karate Club [including Td Hara and James Tompkinson, president and vice-president of the club, respectively]. A young lady placed a garland of flowers, a *lei*, over my head that rested on my shoulders, and then attempted to kiss me on both sides of the face, the traditional Hawaiian *aloha* greeting, to make a stranger feel welcome. I was very surprised by all this kissing, because I had not come across anything like it in Japan. I knew the Hawaiians kissed of course on greeting, but not to the extent I encountered. Anyway, when this girl went to kiss me on my cheek, I turned my head so that I kissed her on the lips – I thought that was what you had to do. One of the Japanese-speaking students who had come to welcome me explained that I had to keep my head straight, so I did. Then I understood. [Not that long after returning to Japan, Kanazawa wrote a humorous article about his first day in Hawaii, and, of the anticipated kisses, that he had dreamed of them 'for a long time and even rehearsed before my departure'[1]].

"That first day, I was taken to the YMCA. It was suggested that I might like to catch up on my sleep, which was very much appreciated, as I had had virtually no sleep aboard the plane. My hosts said that they would pick me up at five o'clock, and we would go out for a meal. When I arrived at the YMCA, I decided to have a shower before resting. There was no en-suite bathroom, and the communal showers were located elsewhere in the building. I shut my room door and found my way to the showers. I had a nice relaxed shower and put my towel around my waist, just like the other men there, but when I got back to my room, I found the door had locked itself. This was also new to me, for in Japan there were no automatic locks. Oh! I wasn't sure what to do. So I made my way to the reception, but downstairs there were many ladies and I couldn't go to the desk because of my state of undress. I could have made a phone call, but I'd left all my money in my room too. I went to the toilets for about an hour and thought about what to do. I decided upon another shower, but after that I still had another seven hours to wait before my hosts arrived. I decided to go to the roof and wait out of the way.

"I stayed on the roof for all those hours. I could hear the telephone ringing in my room, and I didn't know if there had been a change in plan. It was quite stressful. Sometimes, I tried to attract someone's attention below by bellowing out, '*Oss*!' I thought a *karateka* might be walking past, but no one responded. Eventually, at five o'clock someone arrived and I shouted to him below. He called back, 'Oh! Mr. Kanazawa! What has happened? You must please come off the roof!' The student came up and I got back into my room. Then I had to get changed and go out for a meal. I just wanted to go to sleep. I was so very tired, and all I could think of was that I couldn't stay in Hawaii. I got caught out many times because of those self-locking doors.

"I lived at the YMCA for three or four months before a nice new apartment, close to the *dojo*, was found and rented for me by the karate association.

"The Honolulu *dojo* was very beautiful, situated on a first floor, though the Japanese say second floor, in a lovely location – there were nicely laid-out gardens, palms trees, and so on. This *dojo* was to be my base. The students had studied Shotokan and were quite good. I can't remember whether there were any black-belts there or not, probably not, perhaps brown-belt was the highest grade.

"I found the Hawaiians to be very relaxed, big and supple. In Japan, everyone lined up quickly to begin a karate lesson, there was always a tremendous sense of urgency, but in 1961 Hawaii the students just strolled into line. I found this very difficult. There seemed to be no focused intent. They didn't seem to have an understanding of the karate spirit at all. They didn't seem to know how to concentrate. However, they learned very quickly, picking up on the atmosphere of discontent that I generated.

"I taught at that *dojo* three times a day – morning, afternoon and evening, two hours on each occasion. This was a lot of training, and I had no holidays, but I was young and it was okay, though I got tired. The morning and afternoon sessions were not that well attended, and catered for night and shift workers, but the evening class had an average of forty students in it. I suppose the club had between one hundred and fifty and two hundred members. There were quite a few women training which was a surprise, for in Japan few women trained in karate. I got the odd day off of course, but the only trip away from the islands I recall making was to Los Angeles, when Nishiyama invited me over for a tournament, and I took a team of five – three men and two women.

"The same problem with women happened in Hawaii as at Takushoku and at the JKA. I was so committed to teaching and training that I never had any time to build a lasting relationship. I had many businessmen as students of course, and they would invite me to a club in Honolulu where there were a number of girls.

"Hawaii was very cosmopolitan and multi-racial. Many Japanese, many Okinawans, emigrated to the islands, particularly at the end of the nineteenth century, along with Chinese, and others, normally of the unskilled classes, especially agricultural labourers, sugar cane cutters and the like. [In 1960, the percentage of Japanese, including Okinawan, as a percentage of the total population was about 37%]. In the early twentieth century, many Filipinos arrived, as did some Puerto Ricans. Caucasians settled, particularly in the early 1900s, and were composed mainly of Americans, Russians, Portuguese, Germans, Poles, Spaniards and Italians – a pretty mixed bunch. The Japanese even had their own radio programmes. There were sixteen radio stations on Hawaii in 1960,

Master Kanazawa and Master Nishiyama on arrival in Hawaii – c.1962

nine of which were based in Honolulu.

"This relaxed style of living on the Hawaiian islands had the potential for causing all sorts of individual and social problems in my view, especially amongst the youth." In a magazine article of the time, Kanazawa noted: "During my first summer here [Hawaii], I saw children on vacation not doing anything in particular and just wasting their time away. There is a lot of delinquency in the world, and much of it can be attributed to the drifting into unhealthy habits and attitudes. I thought that here was my chance to try to teach these children something worthwhile, instead of learning something bad, and karate would employ their free time and also make it possible for them to learn the important principles of the art ... Near the end of that summer the youths began to show promise in what I had been undertaking. Some of the parents remarked that their children were more mature and more obedient to them. They asked me to continue with the classes for their children and I am happily doing so."[4]

Master Kanazawa continued: "As one might imagine, with a significant proportion of Japanese and Okinawans, there were a number of martial arts being practised on the islands. I was an All-Japan karate champion, and a number of people wanted to challenge me, and I obliged them. These were pioneering days remember!

"A boxer came to the *dojo* and sat on my desk and watched my teaching, my training, smiling all the while. In Japan, we sit on a chair and I didn't realize then that sitting on the desk was normal for Americans. In Japan, sitting on a desk would have been seen as very bad manners. Initially, therefore, I was angry, especially because this happened in the *dojo*. But it was nothing really, so I didn't say anything. Whilst I was teaching, demonstrating, occasionally he would laugh out loud. I didn't have enough command of the English language, so again I said nothing, but I decided I'd have a word with him later. One of my students was a Japanese-American and he was bi-lingual, so there would be no problem.

"During a brief rest session during the lesson, my student, the translator, went up and had a word with him, and he came back and reported that the man wanted to have a word with me about karate. 'Okay,' I said. The American asked me, 'What is this?' and raised his arm. 'That is an *age-uke*,' I replied, 'It is used for blocking.' The American smiled. 'What is this?' he then enquired, and showed an *ude-uke*, and I explained through the translator that this was a block also, to the *chudan* area. The American smiled again and said, 'Who would wait while you block?' I knew what he meant. In boxing, there was no time to block because the punches were fast and continuous. I was aware of this, because, of course, I had studied boxing. I found it very difficult to explain because the two fighting systems, karate and boxing, are so different. But I tried to, stating that by practising basics you could learn to block, [that] 'basics are only basic techniques, but you reach a point eventually when your body can understand instantaneously what is required.'[5] The American then asked me through my student, 'Can you block my punch?' I replied that I didn't know. The American then asked me if I would like to try and block his punch, and so I said, 'Okay. But we must wait until the end of the lesson.' In truth, he was a very big and powerful man, and I didn't know what he had in mind. I thought it best that the students were not witnesses to it.

"After the students left the *dojo*, we paired-up. We began. He instantly threw a fast right hook and I ducked under it. I knew what would be coming next, a left body punch or, less likely, an upper-cut, that's the way boxers work, one-two, so, immediately after I ducked, and as he threw his second punch, I swept it away with my palm and *ashi-barai'd* him with my back foot. Bang! Down he went. It was fortunate that he landed on a *tatami* mat, because the *ashi-barai* was a good one.

"Afterwards, the American was very unhappy and relayed his unhappiness through the translator. He said that I had not done what had been agreed upon beforehand. He said that I was to block, not attack. I replied that I had blocked the second punch on the inside of his arm, and then followed this up with an *ashi-barai*, and that in karate an *ashi-barai* was a block and not an attack.

"I then said that if he wanted a fight then that would be different, because I could use the many offensive and counter-offensive techniques of Shotokan. I admitted that his punches might be better than mine, so I would use kicks, because the length of a leg is greater than the length of an arm, and that kicking was one of karate's great strengths. I also said that my kicks were very good and dangerous and that I would break his bones. The reason why I said this was because I had learned that the Americans were in direct contrast to the Japanese when discussing their own ability. In Japan, the greater the power of a man, the less he is inclined to talk about what he can do, but in America the opposite appears to be the case. Also, you have a saying in England, 'Empty vessels make most noise,' and this is true, I think. If I had said that my kicks were quite good, he would have seen it as a weakness. He had seen us practise kicks during the lesson, and he decided not to challenge me. I never saw the boxer again.

"I used the same idea on a wrestler. He came to my *dojo*, just swaggered in with a large group of admirers. I didn't like it. He smiled, and we shook hands and he tried to crush my hand. I didn't like that either. He was certainly very strong though. He wanted to fight and I said okay. I caught him easily, lightly, with an *ippon-ken* to the side of his chest, and he felt great pain. He rose up and looked at me and was very surprised. I seized the opportunity and told him I would rip his heart out if we fought again.

"Another large American, a wrestler, also visited me. He came along with a telephone directory and, standing in front of me, tore it in two. I said to him that karate's power was not that type of power and I tried to explain it, but he had confidence and wanted to challenge me and so I agreed. We paired-up and I launched a *jodan mawashi-geri* and it was all over. It lasted about five seconds I suppose.

"On another occasion, a Japanese Hawaiian, who had studied Kushin-ryu, a style of karate from Kyushu, came to my *dojo* and asked if he could do *kumite* with me. He was a black-belt and his name was Stanley Ono. We paired-up for freestyle and practised for about ten minutes. He was good. Afterwards, he changed styles and became my student. He was loyal, and a very good *karateka*. He worked for Japanese Airlines in Honolulu. I believe he was in command for the company in Hawaii. He was one year younger than me, so I suppose he has retired now.

"When I went to Hawaii I was twenty-nine years old and in peak physical condition. I tended to rely on my physical confidence for my karate. I believe that the energy in the body is centered on three areas: the physical body – bones, muscles, ligaments and so on – the organs, as distinct from the physical body, and the spirit. They work together, but during particular stages of life, each takes a turn at being dominant. Up until the age of about forty, the physical body takes the lead and the other two elements assist. After forty, the physical body begins to decline and the power of the organs, which at this time are stronger than a younger person's, take over control, with the physical body and the spirit taking a secondary role. After the age of about sixty, the organs also begin to lose their power and the spirit takes over, and the physical body and the organs merely assist in an ever-declining role. The spirit has no restrictions, no limitations, it can go on forever. I believe this.

"I practise special exercises in the morning, in bed, before I get up. When I was younger these were more physical. I would raise straightened legs that I kept together and then raise my torso at the same time, so that my body formed a 'V' shape, though not as acute. The concentration was on my abdominal muscles. Then I'd open my legs and arms wide at the same time. There was never any straining however, as this was for meditation. I'd also kneel on the bed, and put my chest on the bed and extend my arms out fully in front of me, and breathe with my bottom. [The author was unable to ascertain exactly what Master Kanazawa meant by this. He did not mean that he didn't use abdominal breathing, inhaling through his nose and exhaling through his mouth. Nor was it a case of 'passing wind.' It is no doubt a meditational technique of which the author is unaware]. Now I use more *ki* and less movement. I move my stomach in waves so the ripple effect massages the organs. This is training for the internal organs; I always think *hara*.

"After about one year, Kenneth Funakoshi started training at my *dojo*. When I heard his name, I was naturally interested, so I asked him if he had family connections with Gichin Funakoshi, and he believed he hadn't. I replied that I thought it might be possible since Okinawa is a small island, but he said no. He didn't know his connection at that time. [Kenneth Funakoshi is related (fourth cousin). Kenneth's father, Yoshio, actually trained with Gichin Funakoshi on Okinawa prior to the master's move to Tokyo in 1922 and then Yoshio emigration to Hawaii]. Kenneth Funakoshi was a very keen, very good student. I think he was a brown-belt when I went back to Japan."

Kenneth Funakoshi, now a Shotokan 8th Dan, and a former Chief Instructor to Hawaii for the JKA (he formed his own association,

Funakoshi's Shotokan Karate Association, in 1987, and is based in California) remembered Master Kanazawa on Hawaii. Twenty-one year old Funakoshi (a noted swimmer, having captained Hawaii) held a Dan grade in judo and a black-belt in kempo, a system which he described as being, "a very aggressive Hawaiian type of street fighting."[6] According to Funakoshi, there were no Japanese styles of karate being taught on the islands in 1960, so after watching Master Kanazawa, Funakoshi decided to start afresh, as a white-belt, and was one of the Master's first students. He recalled about Kanazawa: "He was a great man, yet very humble, a real gentleman. His style of teaching in the early days was slow and easy, karate was new here and almost every student was a beginner. There were one or two brown and black-belts who had been training in Japan whilst working there, but on the whole this was a beginners' class.

"*Sensei* Kanazawa was real gentle with the children and he attracted students of all ages and nationalities to his *dojo*. It is interesting that in the early years the average age of a student was about forty years old. I was seen as a kid. Today most guys have stopped training long before they get to that age...

"The training became more intense and physical as we learned the system ... Even in the rest periods Kanazawa would practice his techniques in front of the mirrors. When Kanazawa taught basics he always explained everything in great detail. He introduced us to timing and movement with focus. He was an excellent teacher."[6]

Kenneth Funakoshi would partner Master Kanazawa in demonstrations, and they became good friends, going to parties and weddings together. Funakoshi recalled an incident in the *dojo*: "We were sparring quite hard one day when he attacked with *yoko-geri-kekomi* and he broke my hand. He was very fast and agile and used to do lots of jump kicks. This included kicking the chain on top of the kick-bag that hung from the ceiling. He did this regularly."[6]

Not long after Kanazawa's return to Tokyo and the arrival of Master Masataki Mori to the islands as his replacement, Funakoshi travelled to Japan to train. Mori, a very strict and demanding instructor, likewise was to stay two years, to be replaced by Master Tetsuhiko Asai, now Chief Instructor to Japan Karate Shotokai, and who, as we have seen, and like Kanazawa before him, had won both the JKA individual *kumite* title and individual *kata*. Asai was replaced by Takehiko Nozaki.

Master Kanazawa continued: "I remember an encounter with a master of Ruson-ryu, a style of karate from Okinawa, who had a *dojo* in Honolulu. He was about the same age as me, perhaps one or two years older, and he showed a fantastic *kata*, unlike anything I had ever seen before – so fast. I was very surprised and asked him what the techniques meant, for he appeared to lightly strike many times before a main technique was delivered. He told me that the light strikes caused paralysis, and that he would touch an opponent's arm, let's say, as many as nine times before he blocked it. So, I asked him if he could perform his techniques on me and I punched *jodan gyaku-zuki* from *kamae*. I wasn't trying to hit him, I showed control, I just wanted to feel the technique. So, I punched and he touched my arm two or three times as my punch went through and stopped just short of his chin. I didn't feel anything, to which he replied that I was too fast.

"After this happened, I think, because he wasn't successful, because, perhaps, he felt a little ashamed, he invited me to his *dojo*. I suppose he wanted he show me what he could do. I went a few days later and I'm not sure what I saw. He sat in *seiza*, concentrating on an object about eight metres away on the *dojo* floor. The sweat was really pouring off him, and then he suddenly extended an arm in front and performed a *teisho* with his hand. As he did this he made a loud *kiai*. To my utter astonishment, the object moved and fell over. I didn't know what to make of it. I was surprised, very surprised. Maybe it was some kind of trick, but I couldn't see anything and I didn't say anything. I had embarrassed him when he couldn't block my punch, and I didn't want to ask any questions for fear of making him feel ashamed, or for fear of appearing impolite. The man wanted me to come to his *dojo* and he showed me this.

"I remember a funny story. I received a challenge one day from a very large Hawaiian who claimed he was a 12th Dan in Kajuken-kempo and he wore a gold belt – silver belt was apparently worn by 11th Dans. 'Oh!' I replied, and asked him, 'What is Kajuken-kempo?' He explained that it was a general martial art made up of judo, kempo, and so on, and he wanted to see how strong I was. I said that I didn't want to fight him, because my philosophy was not to contest local people because only ill feeling would come of it. If I won, everyone would be an enemy to me, and if I lost then my life of karate would be over. If I lost then I would never practise karate again. This is true. So, I had nothing to gain from confrontation, and everything to lose. 'So, you do not have confidence' he said to me, and when I replied that I did have confidence, I thought he understood.

"Just before he left however, he bought two coca-colas from a machine – we didn't have these machines in Japan at the time – and he gave me one. He started to drink and I looked at mine and thought,

'How do I open it?' He knew full well what I was pondering, and took the bottle from me and took the lid off with his fingers. I was very surprised and also angry; he was trying to put me down. So, I rose to the bait and said to him, 'Okay. We will fight, because you think I am weak. But first we must write a disclaimer that if I hurt you, or you hurt me, the injured party can have no redress. You are very strong and I cannot do what you have just done, it is impossible for me, but you don't know me. You have shown me what you can do, now, before we fight, let me show you what I can do.'

"So, I performed *Kanku-sho*, not at the normal speed, but faster. When I had finished he said, 'Oh! Very good.' But I could see that he wasn't overly surprised, so I said that I'd show him one more thing. I collected two, one inch thick [and about one foot square] pieces of wood from the office and threw them up in the air with the intention of breaking them both, one with a kick and the other with a punch or strike, as they fell. I used to perform this at demonstrations, and I usually went for *uraken* and *mawashi-geri*, though sometimes *seiken* and *mae-geri*, which is very difficult. Breaking the boards wasn't my main concern, but getting the timing right in the throws was hard, for if one threw them up together, they'd come down together. Now, my speciality was that having broken the pieces of wood in mid air, one half of each piece would land on top of its other half. That was my intention at least. I'd done it many times before, but this demonstration didn't quite go as planned.

"As the two pieces of wood fell, I *uraken'd* one piece, and that broke in mid air, landing one piece on top of the other, but the *mawashi-geri* wasn't quite as focused as it should have been, and whereas I broke the board in mid air, one piece fell to the ground and the other piece flew into an air-conditioning duct mounted on the wall, and disappeared. I hadn't hit the board squarely in the middle as it fell, and I had pushed slightly.

"The man was really impressed by this. He thought that I had deliberately done what I had done, and he declined to take the challenge further. This made me very happy.

"On another occasion a Korean, accompanied by his wife and two young daughters, came to my *dojo*. They watched my lesson from outside, through the window, and at the end of the lesson he asked to speak to me. He introduced himself as a taekwondo master, a champion; I think he may have said world champion. Someone had informed him that Kanazawa was a karate champion and that I had challenged him, as a taekwondo champion. 'No,' I replied, shaking my head, 'I haven't challenged you. I don't even know you.' It turned out that someone was making trouble. This type of thing happened a few times. I remember when a Japanese Wado-ryu *karateka* came to see me for exactly the same reason. I didn't know this man either. He was younger than me, and I said I would not think of challenging him, because of his age; to challenge someone younger would shame my character, bring dishonour to my name.

"Hawaii was an interesting place to stay, but there were some strange and dangerous characters about. I bought a nice red car with a white line down the side, a Ford saloon, with a special GT engine, and enjoyed relaxing, driving over Oahu. It was a lovely place. Nakayama *Sensei* would have liked it, for there are no snakes on the islands at all.

"One day, I was driving along a back road quite happily, and I came upon a truck in front with three men in the back. This truck was driving very slowly and I wanted to overtake, and as I did so, one of the men pointed a hunting rifle at me. I slammed the accelerator down, it was a fast car, and drove off down the road. I got a reasonable distance down the lane, and turned off and stopped. I ran to the back of my car, opened the boot, and took out my semi-automatic rifle, which fired about twenty rounds and which I used for target practice, which I enjoyed. I never shot animals. I do not approve of taking life for amusement and sport. I stood by the roadside and waited for the truck to come. When it came, they were surprised to see me standing there and they drove past at speed. After they had gone, it struck me what had happened, and what could have happened, and all for no reason.

"I tried surfing too, which I enjoyed. The first time I did it, I almost killed myself. I mounted the board successfully and briefly rode a wave, but I came off and the board went away from me to the shore. The undercurrent of that wave was extremely strong and I couldn't swim against it. In those days we didn't tie a board to an ankle. I called out for help. It was serious. I was a good swimmer, but I encountered a strength that I hadn't met with before. Luckily, some surfers saw me and gave me a board, and I paddled back to the shore. That was nasty.

"I also went sea fishing. Again, the first time I went out in a chartered boat, it was hot and sunny and I just wore trunks. I couldn't understand why other people wore more clothing, the flowery Hawaiian shirts. I soon realized, for I got really badly sun burned. I was two days in bed when I got back. I was sick. I couldn't move. My skin just peeled off me. I thought at the time that in Tokyo the smog must have reduced the amount of sunlight coming through, or the sun was weaker. Of course Hawaii is closer to the equator and when you are out in a boat on a sunny day, the sun also reflects from the water, so I never did that again – you learn through experience!

"Talking about losing skin, I remember the time I caught a marlin; I fished for them in the Pacific off Hawaii and California. I was being seasick on that trip, something I suffer badly from, and the bait was taken. It took me an hour to get that fish in and it weighed one hundred and twenty kilos [264.6 pounds]. What a tremendous battle that fish put up. The skin on my hands, which was hard from karate training, was taken clean off where I had gripped the short rod. I was the only one to catch a fish that day, and I can assure you that it was a complete accident!

"I had experimented in Japan, but it was during this period that I began to conduct personal study, in earnest, into selective board-breaking, or brick-breaking in a stack. In karate you cannot see the real power. If a *karateka* breaks a single board let's say, or two boards or three boards, then this is a form of the energy, but it obscures karate's real energy release. Selective board breaking can show this energy. Power, as such, has nothing whatsoever to do with it." As the master has noted elsewhere: "Only after you have a great deal of experience, training every day, can you understand the concept of 'without power.' "[5]

Master Kanazawa described the phenomenon of selective breaking in a stack in one of his many books: "When I was in Hawaii ... [I would] place four or five pieces of wood together to form a block, and would ask which piece the observers would like me to break. I would break only the piece of wood selected leaving the others intact. The most common request was to break the last piece that is really the easiest, although if either the speed or timing were wrong then all the pieces would break. The most difficult piece to break is the front. A piece in the centre is more difficult to break than the last piece but still not as difficult as the front piece. This is *kime* – the ability to release the power at an intentional point."[7]

Master Kanazawa continued: "People were taken aback when I used to show them how I put my energy into a particular board or brick. It is a very difficult issue to explain, that's why I demonstrated, but this made matters worse! My energy comes from my *hara*, and I also have an image in my mind of what I want to do. As I punch, or kick, at that moment of impact, I feel as though I am inside the board or brick I want to break, and then bang! I self-hypnotize. I used to do this in the *dojo* sometimes, but mostly during demonstrations. I once performed it at the studios of a Hawaiian television company in Honolulu and it was broadcast [on one of six stations operating at the time, three of which were based in Honolulu] throughout the Hawaiian Islands. [The author has written on this phenomenon, and interviewed Master Kanazawa specifically on the subject elsewhere.[8] The author has been unable to trace another *karateka* who claims to be able to perform this feat, and Master Kanazawa has never seen it performed by anyone else].

"Banboku Ono, the Vice-President of the Liberal Democratic Party, who were in power at the time in Japan, accompanied by two important government officials, ministers, of whom Tokuyasu Fukuda, was one, came to Hawaii during my stay. Mister Fukuda asked for me at the airport, and someone knew me and said that I was the one who could perform wood breaks in a stack, and double wood breaks in mid air.

"A very fine *karateka* who is the same age as me, and who can break free falling objects is Mr. Fujimoto of the Itosu-ryu. Something that he can perform that I cannot, is to *nukite* cleanly through an apple. I have seen him *nukite* through so perfectly that the apple has split into two halves as if cut by a knife – wonderful, beautiful. I asked him how he did it, but he couldn't explain either. His demonstration was the finest I have ever seen. When I tried to do it, I practised on a melon first, and I went right through, but I drove melon skin deep under my fingernails.

"Talking of demonstrations of this kind, instructors of the Kyokushinkai sometimes take the tops [necks] off bottles with *shuto*. This is impressive, but Mr. Fujimoto said that he once saw Mr. Oyama take the tops of two bottles placed side by side. This is very interesting, because of the gap.

"Whenever I broke wood or bricks, I always tried to make it clear that this was not the essence or goal of a *karateka*. As one cannot strike in *kumite* as punches and kicks have to be pulled, I used to say that the effects of a strike could be seen on inanimate objects and the effects extrapolated, at least to some considerable degree, to an opponent so struck." As the master noted at the time, in those days, "The breaking of a material object has been shot out of proportion, for within a few months of practice almost anyone can break a board."[4]

Master Kanazawa continued: "When I was in Hawaii I became ill for the first time. I had a stomach ulcer that I put down to the differences in life style. I went to the doctor, but there didn't seem to be anything he could do. In Japan, everything is precise and ordered, you know what is expected of you and you know exactly what to do, it is structured, but in Hawaii everything was so laid back. Everything the Hawaiians did seemed to take a long time; the meals seemed to go on forever. I felt that it was a wonderful location for a holiday, but I found I couldn't live there. The freedom was there to do anything, but the will wasn't. I also had other ambitions, and I was home sick. I wanted to get back to Japan. I missed training with other JKA instructors too. What were my contemporaries training like, and what was their level? Had I slipped by being away, or had I gained? Had anything new come in during my absence? I wanted these questions answered. The original contract was for one year and I had stayed for two years and four months by the time I departed in May 1963.

"When I left Hawaii, there were about the same number of students at the *honbu dojo* as when I arrived, perhaps a few more. The highest Shotokan grade on the islands was 2nd Dan. There were four or five *karateka* holding this grade, of whom I recall Mr. Ono, Mr. Victor Takamori and Mr. Nishimura. It had been my original intention to open up JKA karate to anyone who wanted to try, to make it accessible. 'Karate must be for everybody. Everybody must be strong,'[9] was my motto, if you like.

"I established another two *dojo* in Honolulu, one at Pearl City and another at a Japanese temple. That temple *dojo* is still in existence and under Mr. Nishimura. Behind the harbour the Punchbowl rises, and this now contains a cemetery for war victims; beyond, are the Koolau mountains. I also established *dojo* on the much larger island of Hawaii. Hawaii [population 61,300 in 1960] had the largest active volcano in the world, Mauna Loa [over 13,600 feet in height and extending about sixty miles]. I went up that volcano and it was tremendously impressive. I saw the lava flowing. I liked walking in the mountains.

"I also established a *dojo*, on Maui, at Paukukalo [with a population of 42,500 in 1960], which is notable for the largest volcanic crater in the world, twenty miles in circumference [and over 2,700 feet in depth, the view from the summit of Haleakala, at over 10,000 feet, being considered the grandest in the territory], and another on Kauai [Hanapepe Recreation Hall], which is a small, circular island [a diameter of about twenty-five miles and a population of 28,000 in 1960] dominated by one mountain [Waialeale, which rises to 5,080 feet] and a lovely canyon [Waimea canyon, 3,000 feet deep]. I used to travel across to these islands by plane." [There were a surprising eleven commercial airports operating on Hawaii in 1960].

In a very early copy of *Black Belt* magazine, it was noted that Kanazawa was "also president of the Hawaii Karate Congress (an organization comprised of five different styles of karate) which staged its first exhibition last year [1962] in Honolulu."[4] The article ended with prophetic words: "A bright future lies ahead for this alert and intelligent 31-year-old karate master. Though he admits he is still young and human and liable to make mistakes, he is a perfect example of virile manhood which the world admires."[4]

"I recommended to the JKA that Mr. Shiro Asano be my successor in Hawaii. Asano was very good, but the JKA said no, because he hadn't yet finished the JKA's Instructors' Course. I apologized to Mr. Asano, and, later, said that I would invite him to England, which I did. [Master Asano, now 8th Dan, took up residence in Nottingham in 1968, where he is still based for SKI]. I also wanted Mr. Hideo Ochi to come to England [in 1966], because his [Japanese] wife, who studied English at Tsudajuka University, taught English in Japan. Enoeda, after his six-month trip to South Africa [in 1965], resided in Liverpool, but his visa ran out, or something, and he had to go back to Japan, but Enoeda didn't want to go back, he wanted to go to America for Mr. Okazaki. So I wrote a letter to the JKA and Enoeda went to the USA. That's when I approached Mr. Ochi. Ochi and Asano were classmates and very good friends, so I had it planned, and I thought that it would be good for British karate, especially because of Ochi's wife. Ochi was ready to come to England, but Enoeda was very keen to come back to England. So, I had to write and apologized to Ochi. Not long afterwards, Ochi [who was JKA Grand Champion in 1966, *kumite* champion in 1967 and *kata* champion in 1969 and 1976] settled in Germany for the JKA when I left, Akio Nagai having already been there a number of years.

"SKI has a number of *dojo* on the Hawaiian Islands today, and recently we had a fortieth anniversary dinner at a restaurant and had a nice meal. I like Hawaiian traditional food, *poi*, and when I was there nearly forty years ago, I used to eat lobster with black bean sauce; it wasn't expensive then. Anyway, about thirty students who had been active at that time attended the celebratory meal. Some were SKI, other JKA, and some were with other groups, but we all came together that evening. Last year [1999], I met the governor of Hawaii who said that he had been a student of mine. He told me that the philosophy of life he gained from his karate gave him a great deal. I was naturally very pleased by this.

"When I went back to Japan I had no money because of the car. I hadn't bought the Ford, I'd acquired it on hire purchase, but it had taken all my money. When I got home, I thought, okay, any day now I could die from the ulcer perforating. I drank *sake*, and when I went to the doctors, later, he said that the ulcer had disappeared, though they took some blood and said that I had had a liver problem. Apparently, I had contracted hepatitis. I remember feeling very tired for about six months. Everything seemed to be really hard, such an effort, even sitting was tiring. I thought it was just the amount of training I was doing, and I never consulted a doctor."

VI

GREAT BRITAIN CALLING

Master Kanazawa continued: "When I returned to Tokyo, I acted once again as an instructor at the JKA *honbu* and at numerous affiliated *dojo*. The JKA was the largest karate organization in Japan at the time. I was pleased to be back, but the high standard of living in the capital, which hadn't changed since my student days, was made far worse by my recent stay in Hawaii. I had become accustomed to a better standard of living and having what I wanted. The JKA was a poor association then [student tuition fees being, in 1962, 'two thousand yen a month (about six dollars).'[1] In 1964, the JKA headquarters moved to the old Kodokan building in Suidobashi, Tokyo, near the railway stations at Suidobashi and Korakuen-mae ['to meet with the expanding situation of the organization'[2]]. The home of judo had moved to a larger, better *dojo*, a stone's throw away. The new JKA *honbu* was a white-fronted, flat-roofed, western designed building, three storeys high. The entrance overlooked a very busy crossroads and traffic lights. There were a few trees on the pavement outside. Inside, we had much more room than at Yotsuya. The usual calligraphy adorned the walls, the national flag, an anatomical chart, a small shrine, but what was unusual was that the single *makiwara* was on the outside balcony overlooking the Korakuen baseball stadium. The *dojo* was upstairs, and whilst there was more space, there were some square support pillars that went up through the entire building. These pillars had to be padded. [The JKA later moved to even larger premises, a former multi-lane bowling alley in the Ebisu district of Tokyo]. I trained and taught, trained and taught, just as before. There seemed to be no let up, no rest. It was karate everyday at the *honbu* for beginners and seniors alike, except Thursday's when it was seniors only.

"There were also weight training facilities at Suidobashi. Some *karateka* used the facilities, but I never did. I have always trained just using my body, though, of course, I do press-ups and chin-ups, which

Welcome home meeting given by Musashi Engineering University – 1963

use the body as a weight, but I have never used equipment.

"One student I taught at the Suidobashi *dojo* was Yukio Mishima, the famous novelist, whose real name was Hiraoka Kimitake. This was shortly after I had returned from Europe though [in 1970]. Nakayama had taught him privately and he was a black-belt. [Mishima started training at the JKA headquarters in February, 1967, and was awarded his *Shodan* in June, 1970. He actually participated in the 1970 JKA Championships]. I was introduced to him and Nakayama asked me if I would teach him privately. Mishima [who was forty-five at the time] practised very hard, he gave everything. After that first lesson I said that I would see him the following week, but he replied that he couldn't come because he had a prior appointment. Mishima was a very strict man who was not happy with the direction Japan was taking. He longed for a return of Bushido, the samurai code of honour. He made an attempt to arouse the Japanese spirit in a group of soldiers from a balcony at the Ichigaya Headquarters of the Eastern Army, but it fell on deaf ears as these soldiers were salary-men, only part-time soldiers, and they weren't interested, and some of those who could hear what he said, jeered. Mishima committed *seppuku*, and then, by prior arrangement, had his head cut off by a dedicated follower. That *was* Mishima's prior appointment, that's why he couldn't train with me. [The Mishima Incident occurred on the 25th November, 1970. The ritual disembowelment happened in the office of General Kanetoshi Mashita. After three attempts, Masakatsu Morita failed to sever Mishima's head, and the task was finally accomplished by Hirogasu Koga. Morita also attempted *seppuku* and was, in turn, beheaded by Koga. The following day Mishima was cremated].

Master Kanazawa and university class before the commencement of winter karate training.

"It didn't seem that I'd been back long before the 7th JKA Championships were being held. I reached the semi-finals of the *kumite*, but was beaten by Shirai, who went on to be beaten by Enoeda, who, in turn, had beaten Yaguchi in their semi-final clash. Yaguchi now teaches in Denver, Colorado. My fight with Shirai went the full distance and then we had two extensions, during which he scored with a *chudan mae-geri*; my *gedan-barai* being just too late. Shirai was very clever in his method, his strategy was good, because when we faced each other he only ever watched my feet; he never looked me in the eyes. By watching my feet he got instant information of my intent, of course. If he had looked me in the face, I believe that I would have beaten him, because I felt that my spirit was stronger, my experience greater. The fight was tiring. Mister Miyata was the referee. I remember saying to Enoeda before the semi-finals that he must take the title for the future. If he wished to go to instruct in a foreign country, he must win. I tried to beat Shirai of course, that goes without saying, but at the back of my mind I was also fighting for Enoeda. I wanted a Takushoku man to win [Shirai was a graduate from Komazawa University]. Enoeda took the final and I was delighted. He adopted a way of fighting that was in complete contrast to his usual forward style, and won with two *ippons*

Master Kanazawa punching *jodan gyaku-zuki* against Hiroshi Shirai – JKA Championships, 1963.

– the first *mae-geri*, the second, *gyaku-zuki*. [Master Nakayama described this famous contest as 'one of the finest there has ever been'[3]. I believe I came third in the *kata* [Enoeda came fourth], but I can't remember

Master Kanazawa withdraws his leg after a *mae-geri* attack on Hiroshi Shirai – JKA Championships, 1963.

Master Kanazawa in action during the 1963 individual *kumite* semi-final with Hiroshi Shirai.

Master Enoeda about to receive the 1963 individual *kumite* title. Master Kanazawa and Master Yaguchi take 3rd place.

which *kata* I performed – maybe *Sochin*, maybe not. Asai took the *kata* title. That was my last championships. [Some competitor details for the 1963 championships are to be found in Appendix I]. In 1964, because of the Olympic games being held in Tokyo, there were no championships, and in 1965 until 1968 I resided in Great Britain, and then went to live in Germany for two years before returning to Tokyo.

"I really questioned what karate was about after the 1963 championships as well, because, although I had reached the semi-finals, I hadn't won. Yet, I had great confidence, because I had trained really hard in Hawaii. I remember a newspaper ran a piece about my coming back from Hawaii that said I didn't stand a chance because I hadn't trained hard enough. They said that I'd been away too long and lost 'the edge.' I believe another *karateka* had told the journalist this so as to 'rattle' me. This made me very unhappy because they didn't know what I had done. In fact, I trained harder in Hawaii than I would have done in Japan, and so I started to seriously re-evaluate the meaning of karate, and I began to consider more deeply why Funakoshi *Sensei* had disapproved of competition.

"Today, competition has taken on a position far above its station, and many students are confused. For a *karateka* 'to do only competition is very dangerous – because you understand nothing.'[4] Competition is okay, it's good fun, it's recreation, but it is not Budo. Personally, I would like to see two types of karate – 'one which would be sport-orientated and styleless; the other a martial art with its traditional base and style.'[5]

"At the end of 1963, Nakayama, Shoji, Enoeda, Iwaizumi [Yamaguchi] and Katsuya Kisaka [who was a 4th Dan at the time] travelled to Indonesia to teach, by invitation of President Achmad Sukarno who had attended that year's JKA championships. Shoji and Iwaizumi returned to Tokyo first [on the 29th November], the remainder stayed until the end of the year [returning on 27th December]. At the beginning of the following year [March, 1964] Mr. Kase, who had attended Senshu University, went to South Africa to teach in Durban for three months [for Geo. Higginson].

"I did quite a few demonstrations for the JKA, some of them in front of large audiences, after my return from Hawaii. I remember one that Satoshi Miyazaki [who was a 4th Dan at the time] and I did at Sapporo, Hokkaido [24th November, 1963]. Miyazaki later went to Belgium, but he's dead now [he died in 1993, a 7th Dan]. I had been chosen, along with Kase, Enoeda, Shirai, Ochi [who was a 3rd Dan at the time], and others, including Nakayama *Sensei*, to give a lengthy demonstration to King Baudouin I and Queen Fabiola of Belgium when they visited Japan in early 1964, but their heavy schedule made their intended visit impossible, so we gave a display for their press entourage [at the Kayu Building, Koji-machi, Tokyo. Belgium television filmed the event]."

The JKA's first issue of *Karate-Do*, gives a calendar of events from 27th August, 1963 to the 9th February, 1964, and there are a number of demonstrations included, and, no doubt, Master Kanazawa took part in many, if not all. This was an exciting time for the JKA, and the diversity of events is considerable and are given in abbreviated form in Appendix II.

Master Kanazawa continued: "At the end of 1963 I met someone who was to become a good friend – [Clive] Nicol. When I arrived back from Hawaii, Nicol was away in Canada [working for the Fisheries Research Board on a project surveying Great Bear Lake] and then came back to Tokyo determined to carry on with his karate studies. I first met him at the JKA [they were introduced to one another by Takagi] and was surprised that he had not only married a Japanese [named Sonako], but could speak Japanese. We went on to national television [NHK] together, on a very popular programme, and he partnered me for some *ippon-kumite*." The programme was broadcast on the 27th February, 1964.

Nicol recalled, twelve years after the meeting: "Kanazawa *Sensei*

Masters Kanazawa and Enoeda give a demonstration at the house of a Japanese minister.

Master Kanazawa, with back to camera, on television with three foreign students. Clive Nicol is on the far left – 1964.

was famous for his incredible speed and superb style. He was quite tall, and slim, but each muscle in his body had the definition of an anatomical chart. He was very popular, got along with everybody, always had a smile and words of encouragement."[6]

Master Kanazawa continued: "Nicol trained hard and we practised together [Master Kanazawa gave Nicol private lessons three times a week, each lasting one hour, for which he would accept no money] and he passed his *Shodan* at the first attempt about one year later [29th November, 1964, to be precise. Nicol passed his 1st Dan at the JKA headquarters performing *Kanku-Dai* as his *kata*].

"Nicol saw me selectively break bricks in Tokyo and after that became my student. He is now a Japanese citizen. He is very popular in Japan, often appearing on television. He lives in Nagano Prefecture, west of Tokyo. In fact, he has a celebration tomorrow [29th October, 1999] to mark his Citizenship and the publication of a new book, and because I am travelling, my son is going in my place, as is my secretary. Nicol still trains in karate."

We are fortunate enough to have Nicol's recollection of the selective board-breaking incident. Nicol wrote: "One day, after Kanazawa *Sensei* had smashed a pile of three old red bricks taken from a crumbling wall, he did something which seems physically impossible. The feat of breaking the three bricks, placed flat as they were on a concrete floor, was incredible enough. Most men could not have done it with a hammer, but they broke with a 'whump!' as he brought down the edge of his hand on them. But that, he said, was nothing. Another pile of three old bricks was placed. He determined to put his spirit, or *ki*, into the middle brick. With a shout, he struck the top of the pile of three bricks, and at times we must accept the incredible, for it was the middle brick, and only the middle brick, that cracked through the middle. There was no trick, and only an audience of a few students."[7]

Certainly, Master Kanazawa was justly famous for his *tameshiwari*, and Nicol saw him drive his *nukite* through four inches of pine boards. This is an astonishing feat, perhaps only equalled by the master's demonstration in January 1966, on British television, a detailed description of which is given in Volume II of *Shotokan Dawn*.

Master Kanazawa continued: "Through selective board and brick breaking, I can show something that is hidden from most people. It is there inside them, around them, but they cannot find it. It is very hard to explain. One has to look deep inside oneself, and then outwards, and I have been able to do this through my study of Karate-Do. The more I have trained, the more I can see." As Kanazawa has noted: "Anyone, large or small, has the possibility of phenomenal power, once they learn to use their body correctly."[8]

Master Kanazawa continued: "When I was at university, I was just interested in *kumite*, and I asked, 'Why do *kata*?' but as I matured, as I travelled, gained experience of life, and kept on training very hard – year in, year out – I began to understand. Karate is about harmony – harmony first with oneself, then with others, then with nature and then with the universe. Harmony is important to humans because it brings health and peace; peace and harmony between the mind, body and spirit. Karate gives health and a long-life. Communication is harmony. Technique and power are harmony. We practise *kumite* with a partner to achieve good timing – harmony. If we practise hard, we will never lose. Now, when I am tired, when my [circadian] rhythms are out because of my travelling commitments, I am able to absorb the energy from students who have an excess. This I use to re-charge my batteries. I maintain my energy and mental strength with secret exercises I have devised. I also use an opponent's strength to overcome them. In karate, if you have practised technique, you do not need to use all your energy to succeed. If you use some of your energy against your opponent and at the same time transfer some of your opponent's energy against himself, then the result is the same. By attacking, your opponent brings about his own defeat – this is karate.

"I strive for perfect harmony, to understand more. I believe this understanding helps in the spirit world. I have no proof; my belief is based on a feeling. I have a feeling sometimes of the next world. I like to show my spirit, through my body, in my *kata*. I try hard every time. The spirit improves with training. I like to project my spirit in space. I like to show it to space. Because I believe in an after-life, I am not frightened of dying.

"When we are born, we are given our own spirit, but we also take spirit from the ground and from past generations of nature, and from the heavens. Through karate training I believe it is possible to create one's own power. With this power you can lock into the sound of nature. I will tell of how Terada and I used to make contact with the world of trees.

"We used to go out at night, about 11.00 pm, and sit under ancient trees. Japanese cedar and Japanese oak are very good for this purpose, because they grow to a great age and become very wise. We used to select our trees and then take up the *zazen* meditation position with our straight backs to the great trunks. We used to sit on a straw mats and sit cross-legged, hands cupped in front, right hand over left hand, with the tops of the thumbs touching one another. We would sit like that for three or four hours trying to empty our minds, but it is very difficult. It is strange, but before midnight there is an intensity in the air that disappears in the early hours. The first time I tried sitting under a tree at night, I heard rustling in the bushes and my heart raced as an animal foraged near me, but with time I learned each animal's sound and they no longer bothered or distracted me. We would sit there, eyes open, and after a minimum of three hours the tree I was sitting under would speak to me. This is true. I don't mean that it would use words, but it would impart a strong feeling that would leave a lasting impression. Nature has spirit, and as we are part of nature we can immerse ourselves into the world of other life forms, be they plants or creatures. If I had a problem, the great trees would resolve it for me. A tree, perhaps fifty years old, might have the same life experience as you, lived as long as you, but a tree many hundreds of years old has much more wisdom, and it can impart this wisdom if you have the ears to hear it. I used to sit under an ancient tree when I had problems I couldn't work out about karate. The tree would say to me, 'You are young. Budo is great. You have only taken one or two steps. I am three hundred years old and I am still looking.' Maybe I was dreaming, I don't know, but I would walk home in the pitch dark, happy. I used to practise this meditation/ communication before I studied karate. I started at high school and practised whenever I could – at Takushoku, on the JKA Instructors' Course, as a JKA instructor. I still do it today when I am back in Japan. It has always proved to be wonderful. Please try it. It is very simple. It will change you. It is the nearest experience that I can recommend for everybody to touch the universal spirit.

"It is possible, I feel, to find a way to make contact with the spirit world of times past. I believe in this, but I cannot achieve this yet.

"I was fortunate enough to be born into a landscape of mountains, forests, rivers and ocean. This heritage is very special to me, for early on in life I gained a sensitivity to nature, an understanding of the elemental, of nature's moods, her changes, her rhythms, and my part in that. Our lives were dominated by nature. If the sun set early, we'd go to bed early, get up early and the boats would go out early. If I close my eyes, I can travel back sixty, seventy years. The smell of sea salt tingles the hairs inside my nose. My five senses move and are stretched to their limits as the sunlight softly touches my eyebrows. My bodily fluid melts in the sea and my hair and skin combine with Mother Nature. My breath becomes part of the sea, part of the rolling waves in the breeze, and returns to the sky.

"In the same way, I quickly acquired a deep love of animals, which, of course, are, as we are, part of nature. I believe, without a doubt, that this love of nature helped me in my study of karate. Nature is a very good teacher, and as I consider that everyone is good at something, I think that harmony with nature is my blessing, and this has naturally developed through my practice of karate.

"In terms of karate development, I suppose the most significant event that happened to me in the interim period between Hawaii and England, was when I took a group of students from the Musashi Industrial University, where I taught karate for the JKA, to Okinawa. At this time, I also taught at the Mitsubishi Shoji Company and for the Arabia Oil Company. Musashi were very strong. They had met Takushoku in the JKA team *kumite* finals one year. I was the team manager for Musashi then, but I also taught at Takushoku University, so I knew all the finalists well, and it was very difficult for me to take one side over the other. So, it was arranged for another manager to take over Musashi in the finals.

"The purpose of the trip to Okinawa was, principally, to study karate methods. The problem was that Okinawan karate was shut to the Japanese, as it were. It was a closed shop. The reason for this was partly because a Japanese university had previously visited the island and there had been trouble. Fortunately, the Japanese Minister of Education gave me an introductory letter that I could present to the appropriate people. My younger brother, Hideo, the doctor, had a university senior practising medicine who had influence on Okinawa, and he too gave me an introductory letter. These letters opened up any *dojo* we cared to visit, which was very nice. This was an extremely interesting episode in my life and very educational. Mister Enoeda accompanied us, and so did Mr. Hideki Okomoto, a former captain of Kokushinkan University, who is an 8th Dan living and teaching karate in Egypt. Also, Toshiko Saito, the women's All Japan Champion at both *kata* and *kumite* was with us.

"We left from the port of Kobe and the trip was, for me at least, a pretty awful experience. The sea was rough, bad weather and great waves, and I was seasick the entire three days it took us to get to Naha, the island's capital. It was a large, general-purpose ship, crowded with people and goods. There were cows on deck, wandering about. We practised karate every day on the deck, though finding a convenient space was difficult, especially with the animals. We did a great deal of training in stances as I recall, taking advantage of all the pitching and rolling. I had to put a brave face on it, when I was teaching, but after each lesson was over, I had to go, immediately, to the side of the ship and was sick. That was a long three days, a very long and tiring three

Aboard boat on the way to Okinawa – 1964

days, and I was glad when I was on dry land again.

"The lack of security caused in our bodies as a result of the heaving of a ship, when normally they are in a stable environment on dry land, and the lack of a steady focal point at sea, can play strange tricks on the mind. I remember a story, a very strange story as it turned out, involving an employee of Kanakan. Before I went to Okinawa, a young man aboard one of our ships, on his first ocean voyage, jumped from the trawler into the Panama Canal as it was passing through into the Atlantic. He went crazy because there was no focal point, nothing but horizon and sea. Despite appeals from the fishermen, he nevertheless swam to the shore and was picked up by the American soldiers who put him in jail, thinking he was spying or something. What was strange, was that he was caught on the American base, and had, somehow, walked passed armed guards without being seen. They asked him how he had got into the base, and when he told them, they didn't believe him. The ship couldn't wait for one man of course, and I was asked to go to Panama to sort it out. Well, I did sort it out, and when I picked this young man up, I could see something was wrong and I had to keep an eye on him all the time. We first went to Mexico, but I couldn't sleep because of him, and then we flew to Miami to get back to Tokyo. At Miami Airport he went off again, and they found him in a special, reserved room. Somehow, once again, he had got into this room, passed an armed security guard, without being seen. That's impossible I said to myself when I saw it, but he had managed it. Then all that had to be sorted out, and I couldn't take my eye off him until we got back to Japan. I was absolutely exhausted when I stepped off that plane at Haneda Airport.

"That also reminds me of a karate story, involving the mind, that is equally strange in its own way. In demonstrations, I sometimes used to place an apple on my assistant's head and perform *ushiro-mawashi-geri*, smashing the apple with my heel. I used to do this quite a lot, and one of my assistants was 2nd Dan. After one particular demo, this student looked shocked, and then took his JKA 3rd Dan, which was pretty grueling in those days. This student took his 3rd Dan and passed, and couldn't remember anything at all about it! People said that I must have kicked him in the head, but I replied that of course I hadn't.

"We were all excited to be on Okinawa, the home of karate, the home of Funakoshi *Sensei* and his teachers, though it had changed a great deal since their day. Our hotel was in Naha, and was owned by an Old Boy from Hosei University. He made us very welcome. Naha is the business centre of the island, and is the home of Goju-ryu. Having been the main port for many centuries, the inhabitants of Naha naturally came into contact with the officers and crews from visiting ships, and what is particularly relevant for the development of karate in this specific area, was China. We also visited Shuri, the old capital, a traditional Okinawan town, and I found the karate here not so heavily influenced by Chinese methods, even though it is only about three miles from Naha. The local town of Tomari, a centre of importing and exporting, I found shared both the characteristics of Naha and Shuri in its karate. Everything I saw on Okinawa excited me, even the traditional dancing. You could discern karate techniques in many of the moves.

"Meitoku Yagi *Sensei*, a Goju-ryu master and a student of Chojun Miyagi [the founder of Goju-ryu] – in fact, I believe that Yagi was named as Miyagi's successor – was in-charge of immigration on Okinawa and he had a large *dojo* at the immigration centre. When people land, it acts as an advertisement – 'Okinawa is the home of karate, and we are proud of it.' We trained at that *dojo*, home of Okinawa Karate-Do Goju-Kai, every morning throughout our week's visit, and we faced the *makiwara* each day too. [At the time, Yagi was fifty-two years of age]. In the afternoons and evenings we went to other *dojo*. We visited three Goju-ryu *dojo* and two first generation Uechi-ryu *dojo*. We also visited two Shorin-ryu *dojo*. There are two types of Shorin-ryu – one meaning 'small forest' and the other 'a temple.' [One Shorin-ryu school was founded by Choshin Tomohana, a student of Itosu's, in 1933, from Shuri-te. The other school was founded by Shoshin Nagamine from Shuri-te and Tomari-te, in 1947. Nagamine, of the Sekai Shorin-ryu Karate-Do Renmei, died in 1997]. We could find good points in many things we saw. We went to observe and learn. Every *dojo* was so different, had something really special to show, but they were very closed. Each had secret training, and there appeared to be no communication between them at all.

"I recall watching Yuchoku Higa, a very famous Okinawan karate master [then aged about forty-five, Higa, of the Shorin-ryu Karate-Do Kendokai, died in 1994], punching a small *makiwara*. He never seemed to strike the *makiwara* twice in the same place, like we did in Japan. At first, I thought he couldn't hit the target accurately, but I was completely incorrect. I soon realized that there was a definite pattern to his striking – first the centre of the *makiwara*, then the top left-hand corner, then the top right-hand corner, then the bottom right-hand corner, then the bottom left-hand corner, before starting the sequence off again. Higa *Sensei's* punches looked soft, but they had a tremendous effect. I realized that I was watching a great master. He turned to me and said, 'Last punch,' and with that he performed what looked like an *age-zuki*-type punch and took the straw pad right off the wood. Then the next *karateka* came along, secured his pad, and off he went. Each *karateka* had their own straw pad."

Higa had started training at seventeen years of age, so he would have been practising nearly thirty years when Kanazawa saw him. Higa's early training had been under Jiro Shiroma, who had studied under Itosu, and, after Shiroma's death six years later, Higa practised under Jinan Shinzato, Seiyei Miyahira and Chojun Miyagi. At the time of Kanazawa's visit, Higa was a student of Choshin Chibana. According to Mark Bishop, both Kanazawa and Enoeda had met Higa before in Tokyo, and Higa had "agreed to instruct Kanazawa."[9]

Master Kanazawa continued: "The purpose of our trip, in a karate training sense, was to try things out, and I remember practising with the *chishi*. I really liked the *chishi*. I felt that it was a very good tool for practice, for it makes the fingers, hands, wrists, elbows and shoulders strong and flexible. Training with the *chishi* makes for crisp techniques. Yes, I really liked the *chishi*. Then, there were the *kame*. That was very difficult training, for the clay pots were filled with sand. You grip the top of the neck of the pot to enhance gripping power. When the pots are full, they are heavy, and we practised the foot movements in *kata* whilst holding them. It is a special type of practice, and you have to build the

Master Kanazawa and Master Enoeda (behind) examine the musculature of Master Toguchi, as Master Seiko Higa explains – 1964.

weight up in the jars over a period of time, which we didn't have the opportunity to do. *Kame* practice makes for a strong stance, and strengthens the internal organs through special breathing. [When the jars are full, oil is often placed on the pot mouths so that gripping becomes that much harder]. We saw all sorts of training aids being used [such as the *ishisashi, kongoken, tan, tetsuarei, makiage kigu, udekitae*], and experimented with them, including the *sai*.

"I remember another Shorin-ryu master we saw who had trained under the same instructors as Funakoshi, including Itosu *Sensei*. He was an old man, about eighty years old, I would guess, and his name was Choshin Chibana. Before we met him, I had said to my students, 'Don't ask any questions. Just let him talk,' but one or two couldn't resist. I recall very clearly sitting in a circle around a fire, and someone asking if he was still strong, given his advanced age. He then got up and demonstrated some *kumite*. He blocked his opponent's arm, caught the hand, wrist or arm – I can't be sure – and countered, just like Funakoshi *Sensei* used to do, and then threw the student. It was over in a fraction of a second. I was very impressed. But the best was yet to come!

"Then one of my students asked whether it was true that an Okinawan karate master could pierce the body of an opponent and rip out an organ.

Chibana replied that he wasn't sure, but he got up and led us to his small garden. He had a bundle of small upright bamboo stems bound tightly together. On Okinawa, this training aid is called a *tou*. He started to *nukite* this bundle and his fingers went deep into the stack. He showed this about ten times, I suppose. His fingers had callouses on the tips. I was very surprised at this ability to be honest. Then he started to kick the bamboo, and I realized his toes were actually penetrating the very tight gaps between the stems, as his fingers had done. He demonstrated this about ten times too. I was witnessing real *tsumasaki mae-geri*. I thought that that was incredible. His toes were acting like the tip of a spear. I'd never seen anything like that before, anywhere. He said that breaking was for beginners, and piercing was for the advanced student of karate. We must have all looked a bit dumbfounded, and I remember him saying: 'If I say, you don't understand, and if I show, you don't understand. What am I to do?' All the masters on Okinawa we saw were wonderful, they all had something spiritual about them, and it is impossible to compare styles and abilities, but if I had to choose and say who had impressed me the most during our short stay, then I would say Chibana [Chibana died in 1968].

"Our visit to Okinawa was also cultural, and we visited a number of monuments, memorials to those who had died in the Pacific war. I remember one monument we visited, to pay our respects, was to a group of schoolgirls who had committed suicide rather than be captured by the Americans. There were many stories circulating at the time about what the American soldiers would do to them, chiefly rape, and so that they did not endure this dishonour, they formed a pact, and stabbed each other. Some other women jumped off precipitous cliffs [there is actual film of this], despite being reassured by the Americans that they would not harm them.

"When the fact that we had visited these monuments became known, when our intent was made clear, a number of other *dojo* opened up to us. One of these was the *dojo* of Kanei Uechi, of the Uechi-ryu Karate-Do Kyokai, in Futenma. The Uechi-ryu masters were very impressive, I thought. They were noted for their open-hand techniques, one-knuckle punches, circular blocks, and so on. They would drive their fingers into a sand box, *jari bako*, and had developed callouses on their fingertips. I remember Kanei Uechi, well. He was a quiet and modest man [then aged fifty-two, he died in 1991], and was the eldest son of the founder of Uechi-ryu, Kanbun Uechi [who had studied Chinese Kempo, Pangai-noon, under Chou Tzu-ho {also written as Zhou-Zi-He} (1874/78-1926), in Fukien Province, China, between 1987 and 1910, and continued

Master Kanazawa at one of the war memorials on Okinawa – 1964

practising until his death on 25th November, 1948, aged seventy-one]. Like so many on Okinawa, Uechi lived above his *dojo*. I recall that he held up a piece of tissue paper and let it drop to the floor, and as it fell he performed a *nukite* to it. Uechi-ryu *karateka* specialize in *nukite* rather than *seiken*. The paper didn't seem to have been affected at all, and he just bowed and walked off; usually the paper would be picked up. I didn't understand what he had shown us, so after the little demonstration I signalled to one of my students to pick the tissue up. To my amazement, Uechi *Sensei* had driven his fingers through the centre."

Master Kanazawa noted, concerning circular techniques: "Generally speaking, the Chinese styles are softer and more circular, whereas the majority of the Japanese styles depend on speed and straight-line, linear techniques. But we must understand that both these principles are very important. And both theories are correct. After many, many years study using straight-line techniques, you [Shotokan *karateka*] may understand that straight, or linear, equals circular."[10]

Master Kanazawa continued: "Another *dojo* that opened up to us was that of Shinken Matayoshi [who died in 1997] of the Okinawa Kobudo Renmei.

Sai practice on Okinawa – 1964

"I had an exceptionally instructive week on Okinawa. I learned that Japanese *budo* is more for mind development, whereas Okinawa *budo* is more practical, still more a *jutsu* really, but very refined. One thing I saw, and I still don't completely understand it, was the way they punched *oi-zuki*. In Japan, in Shotokan, we keep a low centre of gravity and try to keep like that as we go through from one stance to another. The Okinawan *zenkutsu-dachi* tended to be much higher, and as they went through, whilst still punching in a straight line, they rose up a little. I found that very strange, and intriguing. Also, I know the Japanese are famous throughout the world for their performance of *kata*, but I thought the Okinawan *kata* were better.

"'*Kata* practice is not meant for demonstration.'[11] Today, *kata* competition is about gymnastics, and many 'contestants emphasize the beauty in forms and movements so as to appeal as a kind of entertainment for spectators.'[12] Beauty is secondary; efficiency of movement is paramount. 'I think the Japanese only half understand karate.'[13] Uechi-ryu has eight *kata*. Kanbun Uechi passed only three *kata* down to his students – *Sanchin, Seisan* and *Sanseiryu*. They are taught progressively in a structured way, which is an excellent idea. [The remaining five Uechi-ryu *kata,* devised by Kanei and top Uechi-ryu students, are: *Dai Ni Seisan* (*Kanshu*), *Kanchin, Kanshiwa, Seichin,* and *Seiryu*].

"We saw wonderful Goju-ryu *kata* too, such as *Tensho* and *Suparinpei*. [The ten remaining *kata* widely taught in Goju-ryu are: *Gekisai Dai Ichi, Gekisai Dai Ni, Saifa, Seiyunchin, Shisouchin, Sanseiryu, Seipei, Sanchin, Kururunfa*, and *Seisan*]. We also trained under Seiko Higa of the Goju-ryu Kokusai Karate Kobudo Renmei [Higa died in 1969]. I thought he was tremendous. Today, I teach the Goju-ryu *kata Seipei* and *Seiyunchin* [*Seienchin*] to my black-belts. 'In my opinion, every black-belt should learn at least two Goju *kata*, and practise them every week.'[14] 'Shotokan is very good for the physical improvement of young people. When you are a little older, you need to think of the *tanden*; this is more like Goju-ryu training ... after about thirty, you should train more like the Goju-ryu ... The thing is to match your training with your age and ability,'[15] [yet] 'age is not important for someone who wants to learn karate,'[16] [for] 'it is never too late to start training.'[17]

"*Bunkai* is very important in *kata*, and I very much like Okinawan *bunkai*. It is a good idea for black-belts to study and discover applications for themselves. If a student practises practical application enough, then it is not too difficult to feel the intention of a movement in the *kata* despite not actually facing a real opponent; it is then that the performance of a *kata* will be greatly enhanced. One important point to remember is that the movements in a *kata* have been formalized. In actual application, movement, technique, is not always identical; to make it so is to artificially force the issue.

"I also saw *nunchaku* demonstrated. As soon as I saw it I thought that *nunchaku* was a combination of karate and t'ai chi. I knew that I could practice this, and began in earnest when I got back to Tokyo. I still practise today [Master Kanazawa wrote a book on the subject entitled, *Nunchaku: Dynamic Training*, published by Sakura].

"I had practised a little t'ai chi in 1957, but it wasn't formal training. After I got back from Hawaii, I started training seriously under Mr. Mura and, principally, under Meiji Yo *Sensei* – though the Chinese surname is Yang – who had studied JKA karate. I was teaching Mr. Yo karate, and he was teaching me t'ai chi at the Nippon Budokan. I first met him at a Takushoku University competition between the students and the Old Boys, when he came to watch, and I started training at his *dojo* in 1963.

"I wanted to learn t'ai chi because it appeared so different from, the opposite of, karate, and it fascinated me – ying and yang, so different, yet unity. In t'ai chi, for example, you must be slow and not focus, whereas in karate you must be fast and have power. I thought that if I studied t'ai chi I would be able to see my karate more clearly. It was like viewing the inside and outside of one's house, one gets a different perspective of the same thing, and I thought t'ai chi would allow me to step outside. It took me more than two years of dedicated practice before I began to feel the way of t'ai chi, which is very different from Shotokan and the two shouldn't be combined.

"My belief is that a serious *karateka* should not learn t'ai chi until probably 4th Dan. If you think of karate as white paint on black rubber, and the rubber is stretched, the grey you get is t'ai chi. That's the way I explain it. In karate, at least in the earlier stages, you use your muscles, you focus and use your muscles, but in t'ai chi you remain relaxed, soft, and you use your intent. The power felt by an adversary when met by t'ai chi energy is like an electric shock. One demonstration of t'ai chi I sometimes do is to ask two people to attack me wherever and whenever they want, except they must not strike my head and groin, this is for display purposes after all. I did such a demonstration in Las Vegas not that long ago at an open karate tournament arranged by Mr. Osamu Ozawa, who died in 1998. I didn't know what they were going to do, and I didn't care. I demonstrated my t'ai chi form, and when I was punched, kicked or grabbed, my opponents were repelled by my intent. I think people were surprised and said that the demonstration had been pre-arranged, but it hadn't. One of my opponents was from Mexico I think, I can't remember where the other was from, and we didn't have any time for a rehearsal in any case, and they didn't know any t'ai chi."

Master Kanazawa noted another analogy in one of his books: "Although it is not the same, t'ai chi 'power' can be compared to the power of a person under hypnosis. A hypnotist can lay a hypnotized person across three chairs and then remove the middle chair without the person falling. Even with someone sitting on his stomach he does not fall. This is not muscle power. I emphasize that t'ai chi is not the same as hypnotism, but muscle power must not be used. The movement must be like a river, like water, strong and inexorable, but without focus."[18]

Master Kanazawa continued: "My study of t'ai chi has given me a greater self-control and an awareness of movement that I lacked before. I am aware of what every muscle is doing throughout a technique. Time and appreciation are stretched. My mind has changed. T'ai chi has honed my focus. 'T'ai chi has many excellent breathing exercises which are lacking in Shotokan,'[19] and this is good for health and *hara*. Most people who study karate concentrate on the physical side and are totally unaware there is another, internal side, which is very powerful.

"In the short time we were on Okinawa, a local kempo group came to our hotel and wanted to challenge us, and they said that they would come back the following day to get our answer. I spoke to Seikichi Toguchi *Sensei* and asked him if it was all right to accept the challenge. Toguchi was an Okinawan Goju-ryu master living and teaching in Tokyo [since the early 1950s], but for some reason was back in Okinawa at the time. Toguchi [who was then aged forty-seven] was born in Naha, and had been a student of Chojun Miyagi. In 1964, he had studied karate for twenty years more than me [commencing, therefore, in 1932]. He looked after us on Okinawa and we were very grateful. He said that we mustn't accept the challenge, and explained that the Okinawans are like a large family, and whatever happened, if we won or lost, we would have nothing but enemies.

"The next day, they came back, and I told them that I had spoken to Toguchi *Sensei* and he said that we must not accept the challenge. However, I informed them that we trained every morning at Yagi *Sensei's dojo*, so that if they wanted to come along and train, we could not say no. The meaning of this was quite clear – we wanted to accept. We had a very strong contingent of students, and with Mr. Enoeda and Mr. Okomoto, we were confident of success!

"The following day the kempo students came to Yagi's *Sensei's dojo*, but watched from outside. They never came in, and we never saw them again.

"I hope to go back to Okinawa next year [2001] to meet one of Funakoshi's relations, a man who actually trained under Funakoshi on Okinawa before 1922, and who is a writer.

"After my trip to Okinawa, I continued teaching for the JKA – day in, day out, and giving many demonstrations." On the 1st April 1964, the first edition (in English) of *Karate-Do*, the JKA's magazine, was published. The JKA record fifty-one *karateka* of 3rd Dan or above. Of these, thirteen were 5th Dan, seven were 6th Dan, one was 7th Dan, and two were 8th Dan (see Appendix III).

Herman Kauz, who went on to translate Master Nakayama's masterpiece, *Dynamic Karate* was, at this time, in Tokyo, training for his 2nd Dan (having received his 1st Dan in 1958), and he provides us with a record of what JKA training was like at the time. Noting that it was the frequency and intensity of the sessions that stood out, Kauz wrote: "In general, formal karate class(es) in Japan are limited to about an hour and fifteen minutes. Some students practice before and after the formal sessions to strengthen their weak points, or to practice formal exercise (*kata*) or free-style sparring. The class time is divided roughly as follows: warm-ups and closing down exercises – 10 minutes; basic karate practice, including punching, striking, blocking and kicking – 30 minutes; sparring – 20 minutes; and *kata* – 15 minutes ... Sometimes the students are given no time to rest during the class. The teacher goes directly from basic practice to sparring to *kata* without a break. At times they do as many as 1000 front kicks with each leg without pause, and 150 triple punches in the straddle-leg stance (*kiba-dachi*). Also, students engage in free-style with ten opponents, one immediately after the other, without resting."[20]

By January 1965, the JKA claimed 16,190 members, in total, of which 8,500 students were said to be registered at the headquarters. However, the remaining number, 7,690, worldwide, was about to take-off, and eventually run into many millions. A major step in this explosion of interest was an American and European tour organized by the JKA in response to *karateka* wishing to learn the JKA system. Master Kanazawa takes up the story: "At the end of March [29th], 1965, Mr. Kase, Mr. Enoeda, Mr. Shirai and I, set out on a world tour to promote JKA karate. My companions had all been teaching at the JKA and at various other institutions – Mr. Kase at Hitotsubashi University, Mr. Enoeda at Tokyo Art School, and Mr. Shirai at Toritsu University and at the United States Airforce. Representatives of small karate associations in different countries who wanted JKA instruction had arranged the trip in response to many enquiries. The previous year, Kazuo Nagai, acting as Foreign affairs officer for the JKA, travelled to America, and specifically to Europe, to consider the feasibility of sending over JKA instructors. In Europe there had been some trouble concerning Mr. Tetsuji Murakami, and Mr. Bell of the British Karate Federation had written to Minoru Mochizuki [in 1960] and the letter handed to Mr. Takagi. A few years later, Bell and another [Jurgen Seydel in Germany] began corresponding with Takagi in earnest. In 1964, it was intended that I go to Europe, but it wasn't decided at that time which country I would be based in.

"Nagai did not train in karate, he was a businessman, a nice man, soft, and one of his ventures was making karate films. I remember lending him some money after Hawaii so that he could produce such a film. Nakayama and Takagi sent him because they knew that he could appraise the situation far better than any *karateka*.

"We had been given a farewell party two days before [at the Hotel Otani], which was also a celebration of the publication of Nakayama *Sensei's, Karate-Do Shinkyotei* by Tsuru Shobo Publishing. We took a copy of the book with us on our trip. This book became *Dynamic Karate*.

Masters Shirai, Mori, Kase, Kanazawa and Enoeda on the party's arrival at Honolulu – 1965.

"Our first port of call was Hawaii. It was nice to see old friends again for nearly two years had passed since I had left. We gave a demonstration in Honolulu and stayed a few days, before travelling to mainland USA and gave displays in Los Angeles, Chicago, New York and Philadelphia. Then we flew to Europe and visited Germany, Belgium, France, Holland, and, last of all, England, also giving demonstrations to large audiences. We gave a fair number of interviews and were filmed in every country. Many people seemed to appreciate JKA karate, and we were very pleased with the response. After our displays in England, I became based in London and my three companions went to South Africa – Kase to Durban, Shirai to Cape Town, and Enoeda to Johannesburg, for six months. Then, Kase went to Holland before settling in [Paris] France; Shirai settled in [Milan] Italy, and Enoeda came back to Britain [Liverpool then London]. I stayed in England for one year, initially, under contract to Mr. Vernon Bell and the BKF, and then the Karate Union of Great Britain was formed, and I stayed another two years. When I left, Enoeda became the JKA chief instructor to Britain.

"I must confess to not wanting to go to Britain initially, but karate was my job and Nakayama *Sensei* insisted that I go. I had made a success of Hawaii, and had got the reputation of something of a trouble-shooter; my English had also improved somewhat. Nicol *San* was enthusiastic about the idea and explained all about Great Britain to me, and when I got to England I found that British karate was very strong in spirit and

Master Kanazawa, countering Master Enoeda's *oi-zuki* attack, performs an *ushiro-geri* from the floor after the jump in the *kata Unsu* – Hawaii, late February/early March, 1965.

the students were very nice. Unlike the greeting I received at Hawaii Airport however, with all those people waiting for me, when I went to England, only Vernon Bell and two students were at Heathrow. There are many tales to tell of this time, but that is another story."

Master Kanazawa's year, April 1965 to May 1966, is covered in great depth in Volume II of the author's, *Shotokan Dawn: A Selected, Early History of Shotokan Karate in Great Britain (1956-1966)*, which is currently in press. Using British Karate Federation records as a backbone, including all surviving letters between Bell and the JKA, a number of very senior British *karateka* provide personal recollections of that momentous year, and Masters Kanazawa and Enoeda are also interviewed. Detailed personal memories of Master Kanazawa from 1965 to 1968, and beyond, are covered in the author's, *The Kanazawa Years: Reminiscences by Michael Randall, 7th Dan, on a Golden Age in British Karate* (Shoto Publishing, 1998), to which Master Kanazawa provided the foreword.

REFERENCES

PREFACE

1. O'Neill, T. *Kanazawa* (*Fighting Arts*, Vol. 2, No. 5, pp. 8-12).

2. Layton, C. *Shotokan Dawn: A Selected Early History of Shotokan Karate in Great Britain (1956-1966) – Vol. II (in press)*.

3. O'Neill, T. *Hirokazu Kanazawa: Background of a Great Champion and Some of his Views on Karate* (*Karate*, No. 10, pp. 6-8, 1969).

Chapter I – MOTIVATED BY REVENGE

1. Kanazawa, H. & Adamou, N. *Kanazawa's Karate* (Dragon Books, Los Angeles: 1981, p. 17).

Chapter II – TAKUSHOKU

1. Hassell, R. *Conversations with the Master: Masatoshi Nakayama* (Focus Publ., St. Louis, Missouri, 1983, p. 2).

2. Hassell, R. *Conversations with the Master: Masatoshi Nakayama* (Focus Publ., St. Louis, Missouri, 1983, p. 9) – from the Foreword by Teruyuki Okazaki.

3. Kershaw, D. *Shiro Asano, 8th Dan, Chief Instructor to SKIEF* (*Shotokan Karate Magazine*, No. 36, pp. 18-19).

4. Funakoshi, G. *Karate-Do Nyumon* (Kodansha, 1988, pp. 54-55).

5. Funakoshi, G. *Karate-Do: My Way of Life* (Kodansha, 1975, p.119).

6. Funakoshi, G. *Karate-Do Kyohan* (Kodansha, 1973, p.18).

7. O'Neill, T. *The Spirit of Karate: Fighting Arts Interviews Master Kanazawa* (*Fighting Arts*, Vol. 4, No. 4, pp. 33-35).

8. Layton, C. *Karate Master: The Life and Times of Mitsusuke Harada* (Bushido, 1997).

9. Layton, C. *Reminiscences by Master Mitsusuke Harada* (KDS Publishing, 1999).
This book is also available in French: *Reminiscences de Maitre Mitsusuke Harada* (KDS Publishing, 2000), translated by Prof. B. Mathieu.

10. Egami, S. *The Heart of Karate-Do* (Kodansha, 1980, p. 74). This book was originally published as, *The Way of Karate: Beyond Technique*.

11. Manning, G. *Kanazawa Sensei on the 'Teaching Challenge'* (*Irish Fighter*, Vol. 3, No. 1, p. 29).

12. Sakamoto, E. *A Karate Champ and Some of his Views* (*Black Belt*, Vol. 1, No. 6, Summer, 1963, pp. 22-25).

Chapter III – THE JKA INSTRUCTORS' PROGRAMME

1. Funakoshi, G. *Karate-Do: My Way of Life* (Kodansha, 1975, p. 94).

2. Hanratty, J. *Nishiyama: The "Master" Interview* (*Fighting Arts International*, No. 51, pp. 38-47).

3. Hassell, R. *Conversations with the Master: Masatoshi Nakayama* (Focus Publ., St. Louis, Missouri, 1983, p. 48).

4. Walsh, D. & Watkins, R. *Takayuki Mikami, 8th Dan JKA* (*Shotokan Karate Magazine*, No. 28, 4-7).

5. Takagi, M. *Thinking at the Gate* (*Karate-Do*, Vol. 1, No. 2, pp. 17-18, 1965). *Karate-Do* was the official publication of the JKA.

REFERENCES

6. Wingate, C. *Effort is the Key: An Interview with Takayuki Mikami* (*Shotokan Karate Magazine*, 22, 18-20). This article was reprinted from the ISKF *Spotlight* magazine, Spring, 1989.

7. Estevez, F. *The Unchanging Path of Shotokan Karate Master Takayuki Mikami* (*Terry O'Neill's Fighting Arts International*, No. 87, pp. 16-20).

8. Layton, C. *Shotokan Dawn: A Selected Early History of Shotokan Karate in Great Britain (1956-1966) – Vol. II (in press)*.

Chapter IV – THE JKA CHAMPIONSHIPS

1. O'Neill, T. *Masatoshi Nakayama: Headmaster of the JKA* (*Fighting Arts*, Vol. 4, No. 2, pp. 2-6).

2. Hanratty, J. *Nishiyama: The "Master" Interview* (*Fighting Arts International*, No. 51, pp. 38-47).

3. Hassell, R. *Conversations with the Master: Masatoshi Nakayama* (Focus Publ., St. Louis, Missouri, 1983, p. 83).

4. Programme to the 1963 JKA Championships, p. 12.

5. Nakayama, M. *On Overcoming the Self* (*Karate-Do*, Vol. 2, p.10, 1965). *Karate-Do* was the official publication of the JKA.

6. Nishiyama, H. *The Karate Contest* (*Samurai*, Vol. 1, No. 2, 1972, p. 34).

7. Hassell, R. *Shotokan Karate: Its History and Evolution* (Focus Publ., St. Louis, Missouri, 1991, p. 70).

8. Nicol, C.W. *Moving Zen* (Paul Crompton, 1975, p. 1).

9. Editor, *Kanazawa!* (*Black-Belt*, Vol. 21, No. 4 (April, 1983), pp. 54-57, 60-61, 107).

10. Shoji, H. *Karate Kata Series, 1, Unsu* (Fukushodo, Tokyo, p. 3).

Preface provided by Nakayama from which quote is taken.

11. Shoji, H. *Karate Kata Series, 1, Unsu* (Fukushodo, Tokyo). Inside back fly-leaf recommendation provided by Nishiyama from which quote is taken.

12. Nakayama, M. *The Soul of Karate-Do: Initial Move and Posture* (*Fighting Arts International*, No. 31, pp. 18-22).

13. Herraiz, S. *Masatoshi Nakayama ... His last Interview* (*Fighting Arts International*, No. 61, pp. 37-41). Translated from the Spanish by Sheila Cook.

14. O'Neill, T. & Keeley, L. *Professor Hidenori Otsuka* (*Fighting Arts*, Vol. 5, No. 1, pp. 27-29).

15. Wingate, C. *Effort is the Key: An Interview with Takayuki Mikami* (*Shotokan Karate Magazine*, 22, pp. 18-20). This article was reprinted from the ISKF *Spotlight* magazine, Spring, 1989.

16. Estevez, F. *The Unchanging Path of Shotokan Karate Master, Takayuki Mikami* (*Terry O'Neill's Fighting Arts International*, No. 87, pp. 16-20).

17. Walsh, D. & Watkins, R. *Takayuki Mikami, 8th Dan JKA* (*Shotokan Karate* Magazine, No. 28, pp. 4-7).

18. Brennan, K., Nowak, F., & Orsos, T. *Kanazawa!* (*Black-Belt*, Vol. 21, No. 4 (April, 1983), pp. 54-57, 60-61, 107).

19. Sakamoto, E. *A Karate Champ and Some of his Views* (*Black Belt*, Vol. 1, No. 6 {Summer 1963}, pp. 22-25).

20. JKA, *Japan Karate Association: 1960*, p. 11 – booklet published by the JKA.

21. Clarke, M. *Listening and Learning: A Visit from Master Kanazawa* (*Shotokan Karate Magazine*, No. 50, pp. 4-7).

22. Hanratty, J. *Nishiyama: The "Master" Interview* (*Fighting Arts International*, No. 51, pp. 39-47).

23. Manning, G. *Kanazawa Sensei on the 'Teaching Challenge'* (*Irish Fighter*, Vol. 3, No. 1, p. 29).

24. Nishiyama, H. & Brown, R.C. *Karate: The Art of "Empty-hand" Fighting* (Tuttle, 1960, pp. 187-189).

Chapter V – JKA CHIEF INSTRUCTOR TO HAWAII

1. Kanazawa, H. *Seeing is Learning* (*Karate-Do*, Vol. 1, No. 1, pp. 20-21, 1964).

2. Nishiyama, H. and Brown, R.C. *Karate: The Art of "Empty-hand" Fighting* (Tuttle, 1960, p. 9).

3. Nicol, C.W. *Moving Zen* (Paul Crompton, London, 1975, p. 105).

4. Sakamoto, E. *A Karate Champ and Some of his Views* (*Black Belt*, Vol. 1, No. 6 {Summer 1963}, pp. 22-25).

5. Brennan, K., Nowak, F., & Orsos, T. *Kanazawa!* (*Black-Belt*, Vol. 21, No. 4 (April, 1983), pp. 54-57, 60-61, 107).

6. Carruthers, G. *Traditional Shotokan at its Best: Kenneth Funakoshi, 8th Dan* (*Shotokan Karate Magazine*, 39, pp. 22-25).

7. Kanazawa, H. & Adamou, N. *Kanazawa's Karate* (Dragon, Los Angeles: 1981, p. 12).

8. Layton, C. *Mysteries of the Martial Arts* (Kime Publ., 1989, pp. 59-76).

9. Tedder, B. *Kanazawa's Karate* (*Fighting Arts International*, No. 55, pp. 19-25).

10. Layton, C. *Karate Master: The Life and Times of Mitsusuke Harada* (Bushido, 1997).

11. Layton, C. *Reminiscences by Master Mitsusuke Harada* (KDS Publ., 1999).

Chapter VI – GREAT BRITAIN CALLING

1. Nicol, C.W. *Moving Zen* (Paul Crompton, London, 1975, p. 8).

2. Higuchi. M. (editor) *JKA Headquarter(s): Moved to Korakuen* (*Karate-Do*, Vol. 2, pp. 4, 1965).

3. Bellamy, S. & Bellamy, T. *Memories of Enoeda ... By His Teacher* (*Fighting Arts*, Vol. 3, No. 1, p. 12).

4. Tedder, B. *Kanazawa Sensei: A Man for all Seasons* (*Fighting Arts International*, No. 57, pp. 4-11).

5. Shuper, M. *Hirokazu Kanazawa: Shotokan's Ultimate Master?* (*Inside Karate*, Vol. 5, No. 6, June 1984, pp. 18-23).

6. Nicol, C.W. *Moving Zen* (Paul Crompton, London, 1975, p. 80).

7. Nicol, C.W. *Moving Zen* (Paul Crompton, London, 1975, pp. 84-85).

8. Kanazawa, H. & Adamou, N. *Kanazawa's Karate* (Dragon, Los Angeles: 1981, p. 13).

9. Bishop, M. *Okinawan Karate: Teachers, Styles and Secret Techniques* (A & C Black, London, 1989, p. 112).

10. Brennan, K., Nowak, F., & Orsos, T. *Kanazawa!* (*Black-Belt*, Vol. 21, No. 4 {April, 1983}, pp. 54-57, 60-61, 107).

11. Kanazawa, H. *Shotokan Karate International Kata: Vol. II* (SKI, 1982).

12. Tedder, B. *SKI World Karate Championships. Part Two: We are the Champions* (*Terry O'Neill's Fighting Arts International*, No. 73, pp. 48-50).

13. MacLaren, I. *Hirokazu Kanazawa: The Guardian of Shotokan Tradition* (*Terry O'Neill's Fighting Arts international*, No. 74, pp. 13-19).

14. Clarke, M. *Hirokazu Kanazawa* (*Budo Dojo*, winter, 1995, pp. 60-63).

15. Clarke, M. *Kanazawa, Master of Shotokan!* (*Australasian Fighting Arts*, Vol. 12, No. 4, April/May 1989, pp. 10-14).

16. Estevez, F. *Discussions with a Master: An Exclusive In-depth Interview with Hirokazu Kanazawa* (*Terry O'Neill's Fighting Arts International*, No. 70, pp. 30-35).

17. Tedder, B. *Sense and Sensibility: The Genius of Master Kanazawa* (*Fighting Arts International*, No. 46, pp. 3-8).

18. Kanazawa, H. & Adamou, N. *Kanazawa's Karate* (Dragon, Los Angeles: 1981, p. 17).

19. MacLaren, I.S. *Hirokazu Kanazawa – Martial Arts Master* (*Karate and Oriental Arts,* No. 71, March/April 1978, pp. 5-7).

20. Kauz, H. *Training in Japan and America* (*Karate-Do*, Vol. 2, p. 12, 1965).

OTHER PRINTED MATERIAL IN ENGLISH FEATURING MASTER KANAZAWA

Carpenter, R. *Kanazawa Returns!* (*Fighting Arts International*, Vol. 6, No. 3, pp. 46-47).

Cheetham, J. *Training with a Shotokan Legend: Hirokazu Kanazawa* (*Shotokan Karate Magazine*, No. 50, p. 32).

Clarke, M. *Kanazawa on Shotokan and Tai Chi* (*Shotokan Karate Magazine*, No. 49, pp. 22-24).

Estevez, F. *Shotokan Karate in California: 1st Annual SKIF Training Camp* (*Terry O'Neill's Fighting Arts International*, No. 92, pp. 73-75).

Fraguas, J. *Master of the Karate Spirit: Hirokazu Kanazawa* (*Martial Arts and Combat Sports*, Vol. 21, No. 10, October, 2000, pp. 36-41, 56).

Hoag, D. *Hara and Traditional Karate* (*Karate Illustrated*, Vol. 15, No. 9, pp. 16-22).

Hyland, S. *Impressions of a Legend: Hirokazu Kanazawa* (*Shotokan Karate Magazine*, No. 22, pp. 4-8).

Kanazawa, H. *Hangestu (and the ten elements of kata)* (*Fighting Arts*, Vol. 3, No. 4, pp. 10-16).

Kanazawa, H. *Heart, Dream, Body* (*Irish Fighter*, Vol. 2, No. 4, p. 29).

Kanazawa, H. *The Japanese Fighting Arts* (Arlington Books, 1967). Edited by John Goodbody.

Kanazawa, H. *Kanku-Dai Shotokan Karate: Kata No. 1* (Paul H. Crompton, 1969).

Kanazawa, H. *Basic Karate Katas* (Paul Crompton, 2nd ed., 1972.). Edited by Crispin Rogers

Kanazawa, H., & Adamou, N.B. *Karate: Basics for Beginners* (1974).

Kanazawa, H. *Shotokan Karate International Kata: Vol. I* (SKI, 1981).

Kanazawa, H. *Nunchaku Dynamic Training* (Dragon Books, 1982).

Kanazawa, H. *Dynamic Power of Karate* (Dragon Books). Formerly published as *Kanazawa's Karate*.

Kanazawa, H. *SKI Kumite Kyohan* (SKI, 1987).

Kirkham, D. *Hirokazu Kanazawa* (*Shotokan Karate Magazine*, No. 6, pp. 6-9).

Layton, C. *The Kanazawa Years: Reminiscences by Michael Randall, 7th Dan, on a Golden Age in British Karate* (Shoto Publishing, 1998).

Layton, C. & Cook, H. *The Shotokan Karate Book of Quotes* (Kirby Publishing, 2001).

Manning, G. *Kanazawa Sensei in Ireland* (*Fighting Arts International*, No. 53, pp. 62-63).

Manning, G. *Karate-Do Budo Essential – Kanazawa* (*Irish Fighter*, Vol. 2, No. 1, p. 42).

Manning, G. *Goshinjutsu – Way of Self-Defense* (*Irish Fighter*, Vol. 2, No. 3, p. 35).

Tedder, B. *News From Shotokan Karate International: Kanazawa Sensei in London* (*Fighting Arts International*, Vol. 5, No. 6, p. 72).

Tedder, B. *Kanazawa's Karate* (*Fighting Arts International*, No. 44, pp. 34-35).

Tedder, B. *The Finer Points of Karate: In-Depth Training under Master Kanazawa* (*Fighting Arts International*, No. 56, pp. 19-25).

Tedder, B. *The Third SKI World Karate Championships: Part II* (*Fighting Arts International*, No. 58, pp. 54-60).

Tedder, B. *In-depth Karate Training Under Master Kanazawa at the First SKI European Karate Course* (*Fighting Arts International*, No. 67, pp. 46-47).

Tedder, B. *The Shape of Things to Come: Master Kanazawa's Karate and T'ai Chi Courses* (*Traditional Karate*, Vol. 2, No. 2, July, 1988, pp. 45-52).

APPENDIX I

Some Ages, Grades, Heights and Weights of Competitors at the 1963 JKA Championships

Name	Age	Grade (Dan)	Height (metres)	Weight (kgs)	Favourite Kata
Asai, T.	27	4	1.64	65	—
Enoeda, K.	27	4	1.75	75	Jitte
Iwaizumi, T.	27	4	1.68	65	—
Kanazawa, H.	31	4	1.74	68	Sochin
Kisaka, K.	25	4	1.78	65	Gankaku
Majima, K.	23	3	1.70	60	Kanku-sho
Miyazaki, S.	24	3	1.70	70	Sochin
Mori, O.	26	3	1.72	68	Kanku-dai
Nakaya, K.	25	3	1.55	53	Kanku
Sakai, T.	23	3	1.73	68	Bassai
Shinokuma, Y.	26	3	1.65	67	Hangetsu
Shirai, H.	25	4	1.71	70	Sochin
Takahashi, Y.	24	3	1.65	60	Bassai-sho
Ueki, M.	24	3	1.68	60	Gankaku
Usui, Y.	29	3	1.73	69	Kanku
Yabe, J.	23	-	1.75	67	—
Yaguchi, Y.	27	4	1.75	75	Bassai-sho

(Data taken from the 1963 JKA Championship programme).

APPENDIX II

Diary of JKA Events from 27th August 1963,
to the 9th February 1964.
(Abbreviated, and including only events in Japan)

1963

27th Aug – J. Lallee of the FFJDA, France, visited the JKA to see karate movies and performances.
1st Sept – Prof. Waud of Michigan University called at the JKA.
9th Sept – 2nd Karate Championships in Kyushu District – Shirai won both *kata* and *kumite*.
18th Sept – Asai taught first karate lesson at Kokushikan University and High School. Inaugural ceremony also held.
8th Oct – Nakayama and eleven other JKA instructors give an exhibition at the All Japan Policemen Kendo Meeting in Tokyo.
10th Oct – Officials from the Czechoslovakian Embassy visit JKA to see karate. Sankei News came to report.
16th Oct – Demonstration to mark the 15th anniversary of Komazawa University karate club.
22nd Oct – Demonstration and karate movies shown at the Czech Embassy.
24th Oct – Karate movies shown at New Zealand Embassy.
5th Nov – Twenty universities partake in the Kanto District Students Karate League-Match. 1st – Nihon Univ.; 2nd – Toritsu Univ.; 3rd – Aoyama Gakuin Univ.
– Takagi, Nakayama, Shoji, Enoeda, Iwaizumi and Kisaka fly to Djakarta.
17th Nov – JKA grading exam for 157 students – 113 1st Dan, 41 2nd Dan, 3 3rd Dan.
23rd Nov – Demonstration in Kobe to celebrate 10th anniversary of Kobe JKA Branch.
24th Nov – Hokkaido District Championships held at Sapporo.

APPENDICES

31st Nov – Shizuoka Prefectural Championships held in Shizuoka City.

1964

12th Jan – New Year ceremony at JKA *honbu dojo*.
18th Jan – Grading examination given at the National Defence Academy.
– Demonstration for seventeen Belgian pressmen at Foreign Ministry.
20th Jan – 7 day winter training begins at the JKA headquarters.
23rd Jan – Pierre Fannoy, from Belgian, takes photos of JKA karate.
8th Feb – Nakayama attends the winter-training closing demonstration at Chiba Rocket Troop of National Defence Army.
9th Feb – Grading examination given to 106 students.
– Nakayama and Takagi attend farewell party of graduate members of the National Defence Academy Karate Club.

(Data taken from *Karate-Do*, Vol. I, No. 1, 1964).

APPENDIX III

Senior Dan grades of the JKA (1964)

Name	Grade (Dan)	Dojo/Branch
Miyata, Minoru	8	Kyushu
Nakayama, Masatoshi	8	Tokyo
Moritaka, Shinji	7	Kyushu
Kase, Taiji	6	South Africa
Kikuchi, Keiji	6	Tohoku
Myojo, Ryohei	6	Shikoku
Naka, Takashi	6	Hokkaido
Nishimura, Susumu	6	Hokuriku
Nishiyama, Hidetaka	6	USA
Sugiura, Motokuni	6	Tokyo
Arai, Takamichi	5	Kanto
Asai, Tetsuhiko	5	Tokyo
Enoeda, Keinosuke	5	Tokyo
Iwaizumi, Toru	5	Tokyo
Kanazawa, Hirokazu	5	Tokyo
Mikami, Takayuki	5	USA
Mori, Masataka	5	USA
Okazaki, Teruyuki	5	USA
Ozawa, Osamu	5	Kinki
Shirai, Hiroshi	5	Tokyo
Shoji, Hiroshi	5	Tokyo
Tsuji, Kohei	5	Kyushu
Yaguchi, Yutaka	5	Tokyo
Akiyama, Hitoshi	4	Chugoku
Fujimoto, Kiyoshi	4	Shikoku

APPENDICES

Name	Grade (Dan)	Dojo/Branch
Habu, Yoshiki	4	Tokyo
Hyogo, Minoru	4	Kinki
Kisaka, Katsuya	4	Tokyo
Mabuchi, Teruo	4	Tokai
Maruo, Takaki	4	Kyushu
Miyazaki, Tetsu	4	Tokyo
Nakaya, Takeshi	4	Tokyo
Ogata, Takaaki	4	Tokyo
Sakamoto, Masaru	4	Tokyo
Sato, Masaki	4	Tokyo
Takahashi, Yoshimasa	4	Tokyo
Takaura, Eiji	4	Kinki
Takemo, Hiroshi	4	Kinki
Tanaka, Akira	4	Kinki
Ueki, Masaaki	4	Tokyo
Itaya, Michihisa	3	Tokyo
Jitsuhara, Shoji	3	Tokyo
Kano, Masahiko	3	Tokyo
Majima, Kenshiro	3	Tokyo
Mori, Osamu	3	Tokyo
Ochi, Hideo	3	Tokyo
Sakai, Ryunosuke	3	Kyushu
Sato, Yuji	3	Tohoku
Takahashi, Anki	3	Tokyo
Usui, Yonosuke	3	Chugoku
Yagi, Isao	3	Shikoku

(Data taken from *Karate-Do*, Vol. I, No. 1, 1964).

GLOSSARY

Age-uke – rising-block
Age-zuki – rising-punch
Aikido – Way of harmony
Aikidoka – a student of aikido
Ashi-barai – foot-sweep
Awase-teisho-zuki – U-palm-heel-punch
Awase-zuki – U-punch
Bassai-dai – a Shotokan *kata* (to penetrate a fortress – major)
Bassai-sho – a Shotokan *kata* (to penetrate a fortress – minor)
Batan – slam, hit hard
Bo – stick (staff)
Bokuto – wooden sword
Budo – martial Way
Bujutsu – martial skill
Bunkai – application of *kata* moves
Chi – the Chinese for '*ki*' (but they may not be the same)
Chinte – a Shotokan *kata* (strange hand)
Chishi – stone lever weight
Chudan – middle level (chest height)
Chudan gyaku-zuki – middle-level reverse-punch
Chudan mae-geri – middle-level front-kick
Chudan mawashi-empi – middle-level roundhouse elbow [strike]
Chudan mawashi-geri – middle-level roundhouse-kick
Chudan oi-zuki – middle-level lunge-punch
Chudan tate-shuto-uke – middle-level vertical knife-hand block
Chudan-zuki – middle-level punch
Dachi – stance
Dai – major
Daichi Nidan – a *kata* employing only kicks (second level)
Daichi Shodan – a *kata* employing only kicks (first level)
Dai Ni Seisan – a Uechi-ryu *kata* (*Seisan* No. 2)
Dan – black belt grade (climbing from *shodan*, upwards).
Dojo – Place of the Way (training hall)
Dojo kun – morals of the *dojo*
Empi – elbow

Empi-uke – elbow-block
Enpi – a Shotokan *kata* (flying swallow)
Fudo-dachi – rooted stance
Fumikomi – stamping-kick
Furi-uchi – pendulum strike
Gankaku – a Shotokan *kata* (crane on a rock)
Gankaku-sho – a Tomari *kata* taught by Master Kanazawa
Gasshuku – summer school
Gedan – lower level
Gedan-barai – lower-level or downward-block
Gedan oi-zuki – lower-level lunge-punch
Gekisai Dai Ichi – a Goju-ryu *kata* (to tear and rip {1})
Gekisai Dai Ni – a Goju-ryu *kata* (to tear and rip {2})
Geri -kick
Geta – wooden or iron clogs
Gi – outfit worn by *karateka*
Godan – 5th rank of black belt
Gohon-kumite – five-step sparring
Gojushiho-dai – a Shotokan *kata* (fifty-four steps – major)
Gojushiho-sho – a Shotokan *kata* (fifty-four steps – minor)
Gyaku – reverse
Gyaku-mawashi-geri – reverse roundhouse-kick
Gyaku-uchi-uke – reverse inside block
Gyaku-zuki – reverse punch
Hachiji-dachi – Open-leg stance
Haishu-uke – back-hand block
Haito – ridge-hand
Hangetsu – a Shotokan *kata* (half-moon)
Hangetsu-dachi – half-moon stance
Hara – lower abdomen
Heian – peace (customarily translated as 'peaceful mind' when referring to *kata*)
Heian Godan – a Shotokan *kata* (peaceful mind – 5th level)
Heian Nidan – a Shotokan *kata* (peaceful mind – 2nd level)
Heian Sandan – a Shotokan *kata* (peaceful mind – 3rd level)
Heian Shodan – a Shotokan *kata* (peaceful mind – 1st level)
Heian Yondan – a Shotokan *kata* (peaceful mind – 4th level)
Heiko-dachi – parallel stance
Honbu – headquarters or central *dojo*
Iaido – The art of drawing the sword
Ichi – one

GLOSSARY

Ippon – full-point
Ippon-ken – one knuckle fist
Ippon-kumite – one-step sparring
Ippon-nukite – one finger spear-hand
Ishisashi – stone padlock
Jari bako – box filled with sand (or beans, or gravel)
Jiin – a Shotokan *kata* (named after a temple)
Jion – a Shotokan *kata* (named after a saint or temple)
Jitte – a Shotokan *kata* (ten hands)
Jiyu-ippon-kumite – one-step, semi-free sparring
Jiyu-kumite – free sparring
Jodan – upper level (head height)
Jodan gyaku-zuki – upper-level reverse-punch
Jodan haishu-uke – upper-level back-hand block
Jodan haito-uchi – upper-level ridge-hand strike
Jodan mawashi-geri – upper-level roundhouse-kick
Jodan oi-zuki – upper-level lunge punch
Jodan shuto-uchi – upper-level knife-hand strike
Jodan-zuki – upper-level punch
Jodo – the Way of the stick
Jomei – one who does not exist (a derogatory term)
Joroya – prostitute
Judan – 10th Dan
Judoka – one who practices judo
Jutsu – craft (distinct from *Do*)
Kaisho – open hand
Kamae – freestyle posture
Kame – gripping jar
Kanchin – a Uechi-ryu *kata* (a combination of the name 'Kanbun' and the *kata Sanchin*.
Kanji – Japanese calligraphy
Kanku-dai – a Shotokan *kata* (to view the sky – major)
Kanku-sho – a Shotokan *kata* (to view the sky – minor)
Kanshiwa – a Uechi-ryu *kata* (a combination of the names 'Kanbun' and 'Shushiwa').
Kanshu – a Uechi-ryu *kata* (another name for *Dai Ni Seisan*. *Kanshu* is a combination of the names 'Kanbun' and 'Shushiwa')
Karate – empty-hand
Karate-Do – Way of the empty-hand
Karateka – one who practices karate
Kata – forms (set movements in set sequences)

Kataashi-dachi – one-sided leg stance
Keage – snap-kick
Kekomi -thrust kick
Kendoka – one who practices kendo
Kesageri – diagonal-kick
Ki – vital spirit
Kiai – expression of vital spirit; a special type of shout.
Kiba-dachi – straggle-leg stance
Kihon – basics
Kime – focus of vital spirit
Kobudo – classical weapons
Kobudoka – A student of *kobudo*
Kokangeiko – exchange match
Kokutsu-dachi – back stance
Kongoken – oval metal weight
Kumite – sparring
Kururunfa – a Goju-ryu *kata* (holding ground)
Kyohai – junior
Kyu – non black-belt grade
Mae-geri – front-kick
Makiage kigu – wrist roller
Makiwara – punching board
Mawashi-empi – roundhouse-elbow
Mawashi-geri – roundhouse-kick
Mawashi-kake-uke – roundhouse hooking-block
Meikyo – a Shotokan *kata* (bright mirror)
Mikazuki-geri – crescent-kick
Nafuda – a small wooden slat with the name of a *dojo* member written upon it
Nattou – fermented food made from soya bean
Neko-ashi-dachi – cat-stance
Ni – two
Nidan – 2nd rank of black belt
Nijushiho – a Shotokan *kata* (twenty-four steps)
Nukite – spear-hand
Nunchaku – flail
Oi-zuki – lunge-punch
Osae-haito-uke – ridge-hand pressing block
Oss – a special form of greeting, acknowledgement, bidding farewell
Otoshi-zuki – dropping-punch
Ryu – school or style

GLOSSARY

Ryu-un-no-uke – flowing cloud block
Sai – Chinese/Okinawan hooked metal truncheon
Saifa – a Goju-ryu *kata* (breaking ground)
Sake – rice wine
San – Mister
San – three
Sanbon-zuki – three consecutive punches
Sanchin – a Goju-ryu *kata* (three conflicts)
Sandan – 3rd rank of black belt
Sanseiryu – a Goju-ryu *kata* (thirty-six)
Seichin – a Uechi-ryu *kata* (a combination of the *kata Seisan* and *Sanchin*).
Seiken – fore-fist
Seipei – a Goju-ryu *kata* (eighteen)
Seiryu – a Uechi-ryu *kata* (sixteen)
Seisan – a Goju-ryu *kata* (thirteen)
Seiyunchin – a Goju-ryu *kata* (marching far, quietly)
Seiza – formal sitting position
Sempai – senior
Sensei – teacher
Seppuku – ritual disembowelment
Shakuhachi – Japanese flute
Shihon-nukite – four-fingered spear-hand
Shiko-dachi – square-stance
Shisouchin – a Goju-ryu *kata* (to fight in four directions)
Shodan – 1st rank of black belt
Shuto – knife-hand
Shuto-uchi – knife-hand strike
Shuto-uke - knife-hand block
Sochin – a Shotokan *kata* (to suppress, to preserve the peace)
Soto-ude-uke – block from outside inward employing bottom of wrist
Suparinpei – a Goju-ryu *kata* (one hundred and eight)
Taibu-matsuri – celebration party (used in a cynical form)
T'ai chi [*ch'uan*] – grand ultimate boxing
Taikyoku Nidan – a Shotokan *kata* (first cause – 2nd level)
Taikyoku Sandan – a Shotokan *kata* (first cause – 3rd level)
Taikyoku Shodan – a Shotokan *kata* (first cause – 1st level)
Tai-sabaki – body evasion
Tameshiwari – trial by wood (wood breaking)
Tan – barbell
Tanden – navel

Tatami – straw mat
Tate-empi-uchi – vertical elbow strike
Tate-shuto-uke – vertical knife-hand block
Teisho – palm-heel
Teisho-kosa-uke – crossover palm-heel block
Tekki Nidan – a Shotokan *kata* (iron horse – 2nd level)
Tekki Sandan – a Shotokan *kata* (iron horse – 3rd level)
Tekki Shodan – a Shotokan *kata* (iron horse – 1st level)
Tensho – a Goju-ryu *kata* (turning-palms)
Tetsuarei – dumbbell
Tobi-geri – jumping-kick
Tou – bamboo bundle
Tsumasaki – tips of toes
Tsumasaki mae-geri – front kick delivered with the tips of the toes
Uchi-komi – downward cut of sword
Uchi-uke – inside block
Ude – forearm
Udekitae – arm-tempering post
Ude-uke – forearm block
Uke – blocking
Unsu – a Shotokan *kata* (hands like the clouds)
Uraken – back-fist
Ushiro-geri – back-kick
Ushiro-mawashi-geri – back roundhouse-kick
Wankan – a Shotokan *kata* (king's crown)
Wazari – half-point
Yakuza – literally 'good for nothing' – gangster(s)
Yawara – Japanese colloquial name for *jujitsu*
Yoko – side
Yoko-geri – side-kick
Yoko-geri-keage – side snap-kick
Yoko-geri-kekomi – side thrust-kick
Yoko-tobi-geri – jumping side-kick
Yondan – 4th rank of black-belt
Zazen – seated meditation
Zenkutsu-dachi – front-stance
Zuki – punch

ABOUT THE AUTHOR

Clive Layton, 6th Dan, Master Kanazawa, 10th Dan, and Michael Randall, 7th Dan.

Clive Layton was born in Hertfordshire in 1952, the son of an architect. He began his martial arts training with judo in 1960, and started Shotokan karate in 1973 under Michael Randall and the Adamou brothers, Nick and Chris, gaining his black belt from Hirokazu Kanazawa in 1977. Originally studying fine art, he later read for M.A and Ph.D degrees from the University of London, and is a Chartered Psychologist and teacher. Doctor Layton has appeared on both BBC television and radio in connection with his professional work. A prolific writer, with ninety publications, including eighteen books on karate (some in press), and numerous academic research notes, including those co-authored with famed Goju-ryu master, Morio Higaonna, to his credit, he has emerged not only as one of the most productive, but, arguably, the finest writer on the Way of Shoto in the western world. He has also acted for many years as a consultant reader to the journal, *Perceptual and Motor Skills*, on experimentation into the martial arts. Any spare time is taken up researching new books, pursuing his love of history, film and rare clarets, and enjoying the peace of rural life, by the sea, with his wife, daughter and Labrador. A highly innovative and deep-thinking *karateka*, he currently holds the rank of 6th Dan.

OTHER BOOKS AVAILABLE FROM SHOTO PUBLISHING

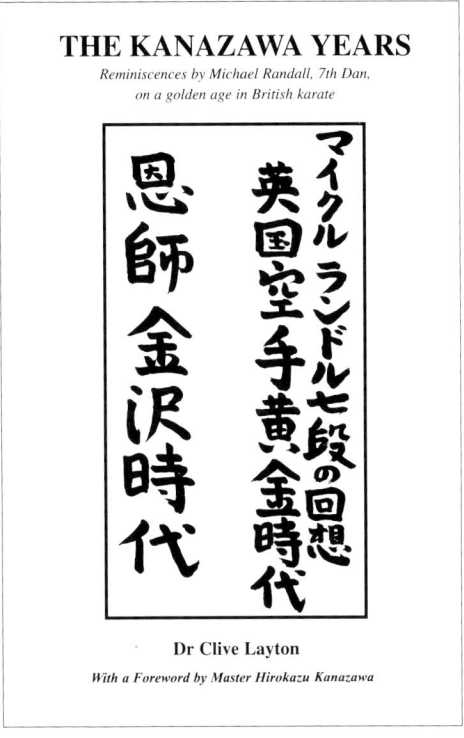

It is, perhaps, difficult for students of Shotokan karate today, to appreciate what training was like in Britain before the coming of the Japan Karate Association. Using the Murakami based British Karate Federation training as a starting point, Michael Randall reflects on the arrival of the JKA's Hirokazu Kanazawa, and the tremendous impact his presence had on the British Shotokan movement.

THE KANAZAWA YEARS thus mainly focuses on the period 1965 to 1968, when the master resided in this country. During this time, Michael became a close disciple of Kanazawa's – one of the Seven Samurai – and was amongst the very first in Britain to gain a JKA karate black-belt. He is, therefore, exceptionally well qualified to speak authoritatively on the subject, and the book is subsequently packed full of stories, often very funny, not only about Kanazawa and the rigorous training, but also of other famous JKA instructors that Michael practised under. The work concludes with a brief "Kanazawa Legacy", a personal account detailing the following three decades of Michael's training, which is seen as a product of those three highly influential years.

THE KANAZAWA YEARS, which contains over one hundred historical photographs, is destined to become a classic, and will forever keep alive a period in British Shotokan history that was perilously close to being lost.

Hardback Edition ISBN 0 9530287 2 0
Paperback Edition ISBN 0 9530287 3 9

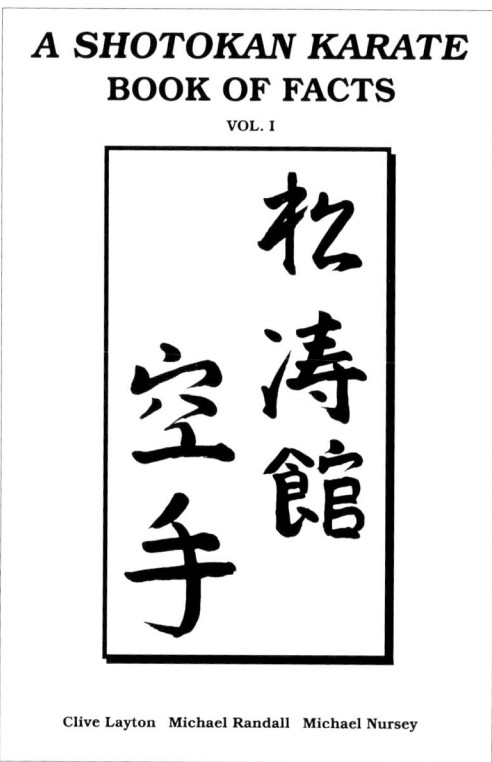

A SHOTOKAN KARATE BOOK OF FACTS
VOL. I

Clive Layton   Michael Randall   Michael Nursey

A SHOTOKAN KARATE BOOK OF FACTS is a valuable, easy to access reference work, on general, historical and technical matters. The authors, all respected senior karateka of long standing, have collaborated to produce a much needed and well-researched quality book, which is considered essential reading for students and instructors alike, who wish to acquire a deeper understanding of their art.

Adopting a question and answer format, Layton, Randall and Nursey have explored a tremendously diverse range of material within their remit. The facts and figures presented, together with the accompanying photographs, allow this unique book to stand proud among the classics in karate publications.

ISBN 0 9530287 0 4

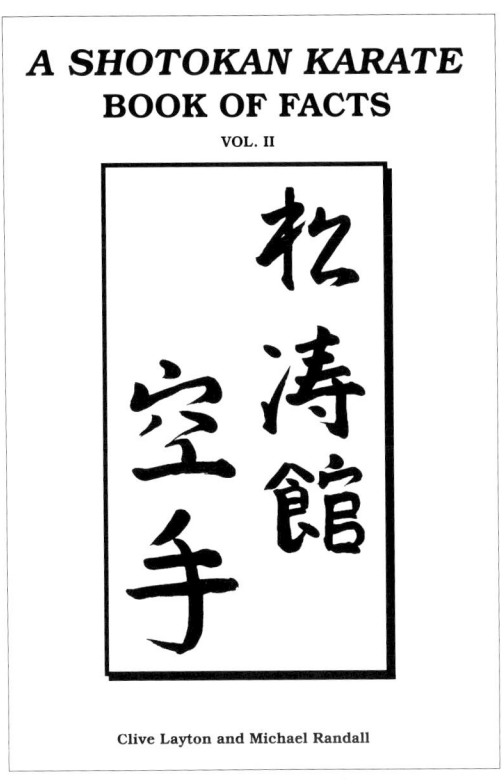

A SHOTOKAN KARATE BOOK OF FACTS
VOL. II

Clive Layton and Michael Randall

In the wake of the success of Volume I of **A SHOTOKAN KARATE BOOK OF FACTS**, this book continues the tradition of providing a valuable reference work for students of Shotokan, irrespective of grade, who wish to acquire a deeper appreciation of their art.

Once again, general, historical and technical information is presented in a friendly question and answer format, and authors' opinions add much where interpretation is required. Also included in this volume are signatures of karateka and budoka important in the development of Shotokan in Great Britain, before the official coming of the Japan Karate Association. Carefully worked out kata embusen are additionally provided, which readers are advised to consult. Historical and detailed photographs accompany the text.

This sequel is one of those rare books that equals the original. **A SHOTOKAN KARATE BOOK OF FACTS** is therefore now, rightly, in two volumes. Layton and Randall have not only made a valuable contribution to Shotokan by producing this work, they are also to be commended for making the information accessible to a wide audience.

ISBN 0 9530287 1 2

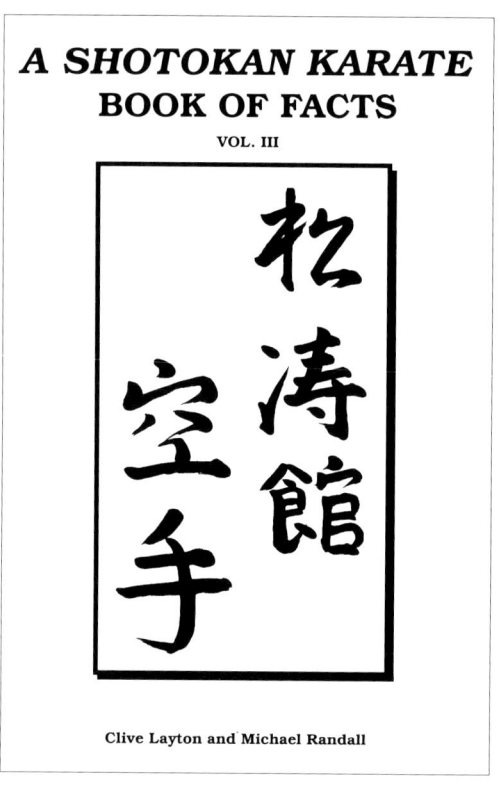

A SHOTOKAN KARATE BOOK OF FACTS
VOL. III

Clive Layton and Michael Randall

A SHOTOKAN KARATE BOOK OF FACTS: Vol. III brings this exceptional and much appreciated reference work to an end. In all, over five hundred questions – general, historical and technical in nature – have been answered.

Features of the present volume include signatures from selected senior British Shotokan karate-ka holding the rank of sixth Dan and above, rare photographs from Japan, the earliest photographs of karate ever published in this country, and Japanese calligraphy. Of course, a whole range of fascinating questions, some quite bizarre, are answered in the same friendly manner that proved so successful in the previous two books. In a few cases, newly acquired information has allowed old gaps in knowledge to be filled, or corrected, and interesting research by the authors, published here for the first time, will open up thoughtful debate. Volume III concludes with a valuable three-volume index and terminology section.

Layton, Randall and Nursey (Vol. I only) have written a series of books that are in a sense, timeless. **A SHOTOKAN KARATE BOOK OF FACTS** really must be considered essential reading for any thoughtful Shotokan karate-ka. One magazine critic wrote of Vol. I, "A 10/10 must buy," and Volumes II and III may also be said to fall into this elite category.

ISBN 0 9530287 4 7

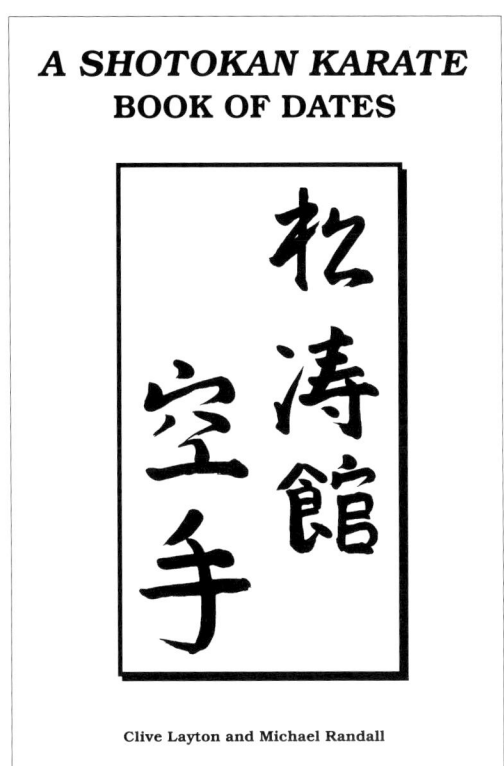

A SHOTOKAN KARATE BOOK OF DATES is an invaluable, easy to read reference work, written for both students and instructors alike. Five hundred chronologically presented date entries are included, generally following an Okinawa-Japan-Great Britain line. Dates commence with the mid 14th century and conclude at 1972, shortly after which came a proliferation of Shotokan karate associations and competitions in Britain, making recording, in the opinion of the authors, often a confusing and not wholly worthwhile affair.

A SHOTOKAN KARATE BOOK OF DATES is another *essential* work from two of Britain's most senior grades, whose collaboration in the past has resulted in the classic three volume, *A Shotokan Karate Book of Facts*, and the much praised, *The Kanazawa Years*.

ISBN 0 9539338 0 6

THE SHOTOKAN KARATE BOOK OF QUOTES

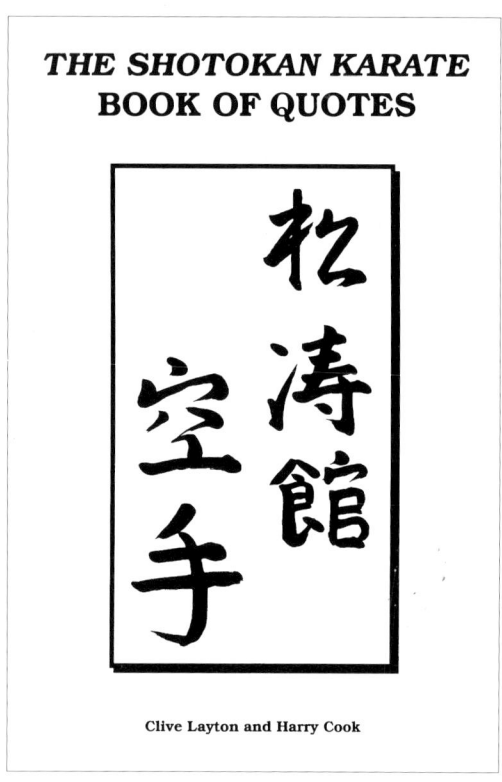

Clive Layton and Harry Cook

The image of Shotokan karateka sharing identical views about the nature of their art is a popular but inaccurate myth. **THE SHOTOKAN KARATE BOOK OF QUOTES** is a unique collection of the thoughts and ideas of many leading Shotokan teachers and practitioners about the essentials of Shotokan karate-do. Using the widest possible range of sources to illustrate the sometimes opposing yet provocative opinions of senior Shotokan karateka of many nationalities, **THE SHOTOKAN KARATE BOOK OF QUOTES** is an invaluable guide for anyone who genuinely wants to understand the art of Shotokan karate-do as it really is.

Hardback Edition ISBN 0 9539338 3 0
Paperback Edition ISBN 0 9539338 2 2